low-fat
cooking

low-fat
cooking

DISHES FOR DELICIOUSLY NUTRITIOUS
HEALTHY EATING

Consultant Editor: **ANNE SHEASBY**

LORENZ BOOKS

First published in 2000 by Lorenz Books
27 West 20th Street, New York, NY 10011

LORENZ BOOKS are available for bulk purchase for sales promotion
and for premium use. For details, write or call the sales director,
Lorenz Books, 27 West 20th Street, New York, NY 10011;
(800) 354-9657

ISBN 0-7548-0552-2

Publisher: Joanna Lorenz
Senior Editor: Linda Fraser
Designer: Sara Kidd
Photographers: Karl Adamson, Steve Baxter, Amanda Heywood. Michael Michaels, Don Last, Edward Allwright,
Thomas Odulate, James Duncan, Peter Reilly, Patrick McLeavey
Recipes: Carla Capalbo and Laura Washburn, Stephen Wheeler, Christine France, Shirley Gill, Roz Denny, Annie
Nichols, Linda Fraser, Catherine Atkinson, Maggie Pannell, Kit Chan, Sue Maggs, Christine Ingram
Home Economists: Wendy Lee, Jane Stevenson, Elizabeth Wolf Cohen,
Kit Chan assisted by Lucy McKelvie, Kathryn Hawkins
Stylists: Blake Minton and Kirsty Rawlings, Fiona Tillett, Hilary Guy, Thomas Odulate,
Madeleine Brehaut, Jo Harris

Previously published as part of a larger compendium, *The Ultimate Fat-Free Cookbook*

1 3 5 7 9 10 8 6 4 2

Contents

INTRODUCTION

A healthy diet is one that provides the body with all the nutrients it needs to be able to grow and repair properly. By eating the right types, balance and proportions of foods, we are more likely to feel healthy, have plenty of energy and a higher resistance to illness that will help protect our body against developing diseases such as heart disease, cancers, bowel disorders and obesity.

By choosing a variety of foods every day, you will ensure that you are supplying your body with all the essential nutrients, including vitamins and minerals, it needs. To get the balance right, it is important to know just how much of each type of food you should be eating.

There are five main food groups (see right), and it is recommended that we eat plenty of fruit, vegetables (at least five portions a day, not including potatoes) and foods such as cereals,

pasta, rice and potatoes; moderate amounts of meat, fish, poultry and dairy products; and only small amounts of foods containing fat or sugar. By choosing a good balance of foods from these groups every day, and choosing lower fat or lower sugar alternatives wherever possible, we will be supplying our bodies with all the nutrients they need for optimum health.

THE ROLE AND IMPORTANCE OF FAT IN OUR DIET

Fats shouldn't be cut out of our diets completely. We need a small amount of fat for general health and well-being – fat is a valuable source of energy, and also helps make food more palatable to eat. However, if you lower the fats, especially saturated fats, in your diet, you will feel healthier; it will help you lose weight and reduce the risk of developing some diseases.

THE FIVE MAIN FOOD GROUPS

● Fruit and vegetables

● Rice, potatoes, bread, pasta and other cereals

● Meat, poultry, fish and alternative proteins

● Milk and other dairy foods

● Foods which contain fat and foods which contain sugar

Aim to limit your daily intake of fats to no more than 30% of total calories. In real terms, this means that for an average intake of 2,000 calories per day, 30% of energy would come from 600 calories. Since each gram of fat provides 9 calories, your total daily intake should be no more than 66.6g fat. Your total intake of saturated fats should be no more than 10% of the total calories.

TYPES OF FAT

All fats in our foods are made up of building blocks of fatty acids and glycerol and their properties vary according to each combination.

There are two types of fat – saturated and unsaturated. The unsaturated group is divided into two types – polyunsaturated and monounsaturated fats.

There is always a combination of each of the three types of fat (saturated, polyunsaturated and monounsaturated fats) in any food, but the amount of each type varies greatly from one food to another.

Left: By choosing a variety of foods from the five main food groups, you will ensure that you are supplying your body with all the nutrients it needs.

SATURATED FATS

All fatty acids are made up of chains of carbon atoms. Each atom has one or more free "bonds" to link with other atoms, and by doing so the fatty acids transport nutrients to cells throughout the body. Without these free "bonds" the atom cannot form any links, that is to say it is completely "saturated." Because of this, the body finds it hard to process the fatty acid into energy, so it simply stores it as fat.

Saturated fats are the fats which you should reduce, as they can increase the level of cholesterol in the blood, which in turn can increase the risk of developing heart disease.

The main sources of saturated fats are animal products, such as meat, and fats, such as butter and lard that are solid at room temperature. However, there are also saturated fats of vegetable origin, notably coconut and palm oils, and some margarines and oils, which are processed by changing some of the unsaturated fatty acids to saturated ones – they are labeled "hydrogenated vegetable oil" and should be avoided.

POLYUNSATURATED FATS

There are two types of polyunsaturated fats, those of vegetable or plant origin (omega 6), such as sunflower oil, soft margarine and seeds, and those from oily fish (omega 3), such as herring, mackerel and sardines. Both fats are usually liquid at room temperature. Small quantities of polyunsaturated fats are essential for good health and are thought to help reduce the level of cholesterol in the blood.

MONOUNSATURATED FATS

Monounsaturated fats are also thought to have the beneficial effect of reducing the blood cholesterol level and this could explain why in some

Above: A selection of foods containing the three main types of fat found in foods

Mediterranean countries there is such a low incidence of heart disease. Monounsaturated fats are found in foods such as olive oil, rapeseed oil, some nuts such as almonds and hazel-nuts, oily fish and avocados.

CUTTING DOWN ON FATS AND SATURATED FATS IN THE DIET

About one quarter of the fat we eat comes from meat and meat products, one-fifth from dairy products and margarine and the rest from breads, biscuits, pastries and other foods. It is easy to cut down on obvious sources of fat in the diet, such as butter, oils, margarine, cream, whole milk and high fat cheese, but we also need to know

about – and watch out for – "hidden" fats. Hidden fats can be found in foods such as cakes, biscuits and nuts. Even lean, trimmed red meats may contain as much as 10% fat.

By being aware of foods which are high in fats and particularly saturated fats, and by making simple changes to your diet, you can reduce the total fat content of your diet quite considerably. Whenever possible, choose reduced fat or low fat alternatives to foods, such as milk, cheese and salad dressings, and fill up on very low fat foods, such as fruit and vegetables, and foods that are high in carbohydrate such as pasta, rice, bread and potatoes.

EASY WAYS TO CUT DOWN FAT AND SATURATED FAT IN THE DAILY DIET

There are lots of simple no-fuss ways of reducing the fat in your diet. Just follow the simple "eat less – try instead" suggestions below to discover how easy it is.

● EAT LESS – Butter, margarine and hard fats.

● TRY INSTEAD – Low fat spread, very low fat spread or polyunsaturated margarine. If you must use butter or solid margarine, make sure they are softened at room temperature and spread them very thinly. Better still, use fat-free spreads such as low fat soft cheese, reduced sugar jams or marmalades for sandwiches and toast.

● EAT LESS – Fatty meats and high fat products such as meat pâtés, hot pies and sausages.

● TRY INSTEAD – Low fat meats, such as chicken and turkey.

Use only the leanest cuts of such meats as lamb, beef and pork.

Always cut any visible fat and skin from meat before cooking.

Choose reduced fat sausages and meat products and eat fish more often.

Try using low fat protein products such as tofu in place of meat in savory recipes.

Make gravies using vegetable water or fat-free stock rather than using meat juices.

● EAT LESS – Full fat dairy products such as whole milk, cream, butter, hard margarine, sour cream, whole milk yogurts and hard cheese.

● TRY INSTEAD – Low fat or skim milk and milk products, low fat yogurts, low fat ricotta cheese and low fat soft cheeses, reduced fat hard cheeses such as Cheddar, and reduced fat creams and sour cream.

● EAT LESS – Solid cooking fats, such as lard or solid margarine.

● TRY INSTEAD – Polyunsaturated or monounsaturated oils, such as olive, sunflower or corn for cooking.

● EAT LESS – Rich salad dressings with full-fat mayonnaise, Thousand Island dressing or French dressing.

● TRY INSTEAD – Reduced fat or fat-free mayonnaise or dressings. Make salad dressings at home with low fat yogurt or ricotta cheese.

● EAT LESS – Fried foods.

● TRY INSTEAD – Fat-free cooking methods such as broiling, microwaving, steaming or baking whenever possible.

Try cooking in a nonstick wok with only a very small amount of oil.

Always roast or broil meat or poultry on a rack.

● EAT LESS – Deep-fried French fries and sautéed potatoes.

● TRY INSTEAD – Fat-free starchy foods such as pasta, couscous and rice. Choose baked or boiled potatoes.

● EAT LESS – Added fat in cooking.

● TRY INSTEAD – To cook with little or no fat. Use heavy or good quality nonstick pans, so that the food doesn't stick.

Try using a small amount of spray oil in cooking to control exactly how much fat you are using.

Use fat-free or low fat ingredients for cooking, such as fruit juice, low fat or fat-free stock, wine or even beer.

● EAT LESS – High fat snacks such as crisps, tortilla chips, fried snacks and pastries, chocolate cakes, muffins, doughnuts, sweet pastries and cookies – especially chocolate ones!

● TRY INSTEAD – Low fat and fat-free fresh or dried fruits, breadsticks or vegetable sticks.

Make your own home-baked low fat cakes and bakes.

If you do buy ready-made cakes and cookies, always choose low fat and reduced fat versions.

FAT-FREE COOKING METHODS

It's very easy to cook without fat – whenever possible, broil, bake, microwave or steam foods without the addition of fat, or try stir-frying without fat – use a little low fat or fat-free stock, wine or fruit juice instead.

● Working with heavy or good quality cookware, you'll find that the amount of fat needed for cooking foods can be kept to an absolute minimum. When making stews or meat sauces such as bolognese, dry-fry the meat to brown it and then drain off all the excess fat before adding the other ingredients. If you do need a little fat for cooking, choose an oil which is high in unsaturates such as corn, sunflower or olive oil and always use as little as possible.

● When baking low fat cakes and bakes, use good quality bakeware which doesn't need greasing before use, or use nonstick parchment paper and only lightly grease before lining.

● Look out for nonstick coated fabric sheet. This re-usable nonstick material is amazingly versatile, it can be cut to size and used to line cake pans, baking sheets or frying pans. Heat resistant up to 550°F and microwave safe, it will last for up to 5 years.

● When baking foods such as chicken or fish, rather than adding a pat of butter to the food, try baking the food in a loosely sealed package of foil or greaseproof paper and adding some wine or fruit juice and herbs or spices to the food before sealing the package.

● When broiling foods, the addition of fat is often unnecessary. If the food shows signs of drying, lightly brush with a small amount of unsaturated oil such as sunflower or corn oil.

Above: Invest in a few of these useful items of cookware for easy fat-free cooking: nonstick cookware and accurate measuring equipment are essential.

● Microwaved foods rarely need the addition of fat, so add herbs or spices for extra flavor and color.

● Steaming or boiling are easy, fat-free ways of cooking many foods, especially vegetables, fish and chicken.

● Try poaching foods, such as chicken, fish and fruit, in stock or syrup – it is another easy, fat-free cooking method.

● Try braising vegetables in the oven in low fat or fat-free stock, wine or simply water with the addition of some herbs.

● Sauté vegetables in low fat or fat-free stock, wine or fruit juice instead of fat or oil.

● Cook vegetables in a covered saucepan over low heat with a little water so they cook in their own juices.

● Marinate food such as meat or poultry in mixtures of alcohol, herbs or spices, and vinegar or fruit juice. This will help to tenderize the meat and add flavor and color and, in addition, the marinade can be used to baste the food while it is cooking.

● When serving vegetables such as boiled potatoes, carrots or peas, resist the temptation to add a pat of butter or margarine. Instead, sprinkle with chopped fresh herbs or ground spices.

COOKING WITH LOW FAT OR NON-FAT INGREDIENTS

Nowadays many foods are available in full fat and reduced fat or very low fat forms. In every supermarket you'll find a huge array of low fat dairy products, such as milk, cream, yogurt, hard and soft cheeses and ricotta cheese; reduced fat sweet or chocolate cookies; reduced fat or fat-free salad dressings and mayonnaise; reduced fat chips and snacks; low fat, half-fat or very low fat spreads; as well as such reduced fat ready-made food products as desserts.

Other foods, such as fresh fruit and vegetables, pasta, rice, potatoes and bread, naturally contain very little fat. Some foods, such as soy sauce, wine, cider, sherry, sugar, honey, syrup and jam, contain no fat at all. By combining these and other low fat foods you can create delicious dishes which contain very little fat.

Some low fat or reduced fat ingredients and products work better than others in cooking, but often a simple substitution of one for another will work. The addition of low fat or non-fat ingredients, such as herbs and spices, also add plenty of extra flavor and color to recipes.

LOW FAT SPREADS IN COOKING

There is a huge variety of low fat, reduced fat and half-fat spreads available in our supermarkets, along with some spreads that are very low in fat. Some are suitable for cooking, while others are suitable only for spreading.

Generally speaking, the very low fat spreads with a fat content of around 20% or less have a high water content and so are unsuitable for cooking and are suitable only for spreading.

Low fat or half-fat spreads with a fat content of around 40% are suitable for spreading and can be used for some cooking methods. They are suitable for recipes such as all-in-one cake and biscuit recipes, all-in-one sauce recipes, sautéing vegetables over low heat, choux pastry and some cake frostings.

When using these low fat spreads for cooking, the fat may behave slightly differently to full fat products such as butter or margarine.

With some recipes, the cooked result may be slightly different, but will still be very acceptable. Other recipes will be just as tasty and successful. For example, choux pastry made using half- or low fat spread is often slightly crisper and lighter in texture than traditional choux pastry, and a cheesecake cookie crust made with melted half- or low fat spread combined with crushed cookie crumbs, may be slightly softer in texture and less crispy than a cookie crust made using melted butter.

When heating half- or low fat spreads, never cook them over high heat. Always use a heavy pan over low heat to avoid the product burning, spitting or spoiling, and stir all the time. With all-in-one sauces, the mixture should be whisked continuously over low heat.

Half-fat or low fat spreads are not suitable for shallow or deep-fat frying, pastry making, rich fruit cakes, some cookies, shortcake, clarified butter and preserves such as lemon curd.

Remember that the storage times for recipes made using half- or low fat spreads may be reduced slightly, because of the lower fat content.

Almost all dairy products now come in low fat or reduced fat versions.

Another way to reduce the fat content of recipes, particularly cake recipes is to use a fruit purée in place of all or some of the fat in a recipe.

Many cake recipes work well using this method, but others may not be so successful. Pastry does not work well. Breads work very well, perhaps because the amount of fat is usually relatively small, as do some cookies and bars, such as brownies and flapjacks.

To make the dried fruit purée to use in recipes, chop 4 ounces ready-to-eat dried fruit and place in a blender or food processor with 5 tablespoons water and blend to a roughly smooth purée. Then, simply substitute the same weight of this dried fruit purée for all or just some of the amount of fat in the recipe. The purée will keep in the fridge for up to three days.

You can use prunes, dried apricots, dried peaches, or dried apples, or substitute mashed fresh fruit, such as ripe bananas or lightly cooked apples, without the added water.

Above: A selection of cooking oils and low fat spreads. Always check the packaging of low fat spreads – for cooking, they must have a fat content of about 40%.

LOW FAT AND VERY LOW FAT SNACKS

Instead of reaching for some chips, a high fat cookie or a chocolate bar when hunger strikes, choose one of these tasty low fat snacks to fill that hungry hole.

● A piece of fresh fruit or vegetable such as an apple, banana or carrot – keep chunks or sticks wrapped in a plastic bag in the fridge.

● Fresh fruit or vegetable chunks – skewer them on to toothpicks or short bamboo skewers to make them into mini kebabs.

● A handful of dried fruit such as raisins, apricots or sultanas. These also make a perfect addition to children's lunch boxes or to school break snacks.

● A portion of canned fruit in natural fruit juice – serve with a spoonful or two of fat-free yogurt.

● One or two crisp rice cakes – delicious on their own, or topped with honey, or reduced fat cheese.

● Crackers, such as water biscuits or crisp breads, spread with reduced sugar jam or marmalade.

● A bowl of whole-wheat breakfast cereal or no-added-sugar granola served with a little skimmed milk.

● Very low fat plain or fruit yogurt or ricotta cheese.

● A toasted teacake spread with reduced sugar jam or marmalade.

● Toasted pancake spread with fruit purée.

THE FAT AND CALORIE CONTENTS OF FOOD

The following figures show the weight of fat (g) and the energy content per 100g/4oz of each food.

VEGETABLES

	FAT (g)	ENERGY		FAT (g)	ENERGY
Broccoli	0.9	33 Kcals/138 kJ	Peas	1.5	83 Kcals/344 kJ
Cabbage	0.4	26 Kcals/109 kJ	Potatoes	0.2	75 Kcals/318 kJ
Carrots	0.3	35 Kcals/146 kJ	Fries, homemade	6.7	189 Kcals/796 kJ
Cauliflower	0.9	34 Kcals/142 kJ	Fries, retail	12.4	239 Kcals/1001 kJ
Cucumber	0.1	10 Kcals/40 kJ	Oven-chips, frozen, baked	4.2	162 Kcals/687 kJ
Mushrooms	0.5	13 Kcals/55 kJ	Tomatoes	0.3	17 Kcals/73 kJ
Onions	0.2	36 Kcals/151 kJ	Zucchini	0.4	18 Kcals/74 kJ

BEANS AND PULSES

	FAT (g)	ENERGY		FAT (g)	ENERGY
Black-eyed peas, cooked	1.8	116 Kcals/494 kJ	Lima beans, canned	0.5	77 Kcals/327 kJ
Chickpeas, canned	2.9	115 Kcals/487 kJ	Red kidney beans, canned	0.6	100 Kcals/424 kJ
Hummus	12.6	187 Kcals/781 kJ	Red lentils, cooked	0.4	100 Kcals/424 kJ

FISH AND SEAFOOD

	FAT (g)	ENERGY		FAT (g)	ENERGY
Cod fillets, fresh	0.7	80 Kcals/337 kJ	Shrimp	0.9	99 Kcals/418 kJ
Crab, canned	0.5	77 Kcals/326 kJ	Trout, grilled	5.4	135 Kcals/565 kJ
Haddock, fresh	0.6	81 Kcals/345 kJ	Tuna, canned in water	0.6	99 Kcals/422 kJ
Lemon sole, fresh	1.5	83 Kcals/351 kJ	Tuna, canned in oil	9.0	189 Kcals/794 kJ

MEAT PRODUCTS

	FAT (g)	ENERGY		FAT (g)	ENERGY
Bacon strip	39.5	414 Kcals/1710 kJ	Chicken fillet, raw	1.1	106 Kcals/449 kJ
Turkey bacon strip	1.0	99 Kcals/414 kJ	Chicken, roasted	12.5	218 Kcals/910 kJ
Beef, ground, raw	16.2	225 Kcals/934 kJ	Duck, meat only, raw	6.5	137 Kcals/575 kJ
Beef, ground, extra lean, raw	9.6	174 Kcals/728 kJ	Duck, roasted, meat, fat and skin	38.1	423 Kcals/1750 kJ
Rump steak, lean and marbled	10.1	174 Kcals/726 kJ	Turkey, meat only, raw	1.6	105 Kcals/443 kJ
Rump steak, lean only	4.1	125 Kcals/526 kJ	Liver, lamb, raw	6.2	137 Kcals/575 kJ
Lamb chops, loin, lean and fat	23.0	277 Kcals/1150 kJ	Salami	45.2	491 Kcals/2031 kJ
Lamb, average, lean, raw	8.3	156 Kcals/651 kJ	Sausage roll, flaky pastry	36.4	477 Kcals/1985 kJ
Pork chops, loin, lean and fat	21.7	270 Kcals/1119 kJ			
Pork, average, lean, raw	4.0	123 Kcals/519 kJ			

DAIRY, FATS AND OILS

	FAT (g)	ENERGY		FAT (g)	ENERGY
Cream, heavy	48.0	449 Kcals/1849 kJ	Greek yogurt	9.1	115 Kcals/477 kJ
Cream, light	19.1	198 Kcals/817 kJ	Reduced fat Greek yogurt	5.0	80 Kcals/335 kJ
Cream, whipping	39.3	373 Kcals/1539 kJ	Butter	81.7	737 Kcals/3031 kJ
Crème fraîche	40.0	379 Kcals/156 kJ	Margarine	81.6	739 Kcals/3039 kJ
Reduced fat crème fraîche	15.0	165 Kcals/683 kJ	Low fat spread	40.5	390 Kcals/1605 kJ
Reduced fat heavy cream	24.0	243 Kcals/1002 kJ	Very low fat spread	25	273 Kcals/1128 kJ
Milk, skim	0.1	33 Kcals/130 kJ	Shortening	99.0	891 Kcals/3663 kJ
Milk, whole	3.9	66 Kcals/275 kJ	Corn oil	99.9	899 Kcals/3696 kJ
Brie	26.9	319 Kcals/1323 kJ	Olive oil	99.9	899 Kcals/3696 kJ
Cheddar cheese	34.4	412 Kcals/1708 kJ	Safflower oil	99.9	899 Kcals/3696 kJ
Cheddar-type, reduced fat	15.0	261 Kcals/1091 kJ	Eggs	10.8	147 Kcals/612 kJ
Cream cheese	47.4	439 Kcals/1807 kJ	Egg yolk	30.5	339 Kcals/1402 kJ
Skimmed milk soft cheese	Trace	74 Kcals/313 kJ	Egg white	Trace	36 Kcals/153 kJ
Edam cheese	25.4	333 Kcals/1382 kJ	Fat-free dressing	1.2	67 Kcals/282 kJ
Feta cheese	20.2	250 Kcals/1037 kJ	French dressing	49.4	462 Kcals/1902 kJ
Parmesan cheese	32.7	452 Kcals/1880 kJ	Mayonnaise	75.6	691 Kcals2843 kJ
Low fat yogurt, plain	0.8	56 Kcals/236 kJ	Mayonnaise, reduced calorie	28.1	288 Kcals/1188 kJ

CEREALS, BAKING AND PRESERVES

	FAT (g)	ENERGY		FAT (g)	ENERGY
Brown rice, uncooked	2.8	357 Kcals/1518 kJ	Flapjack	26.6	484 Kcals/2028 kJ
White rice, uncooked	3.6	383 K cals/1630 kJ	Shortcake	26.1	498 Kcals/2087 kJ
Pasta, white, uncooked	1.8	342 Kcals/1456 kJ	Spongecake	16.9	393 Kcals/1652 kJ
Pasta, whole-wheat, uncooked	2.5	324 Kcal/1379 kJ	Fatless spongecake	6.1	294 Kcals/1245 kJ
Brown bread	2.0	218 Kcals/927 kJ	Doughnut, jelly	14.5	336 Kcals/1414 kJ
White bread	1.9	235 Kcals/1002 kJ	Sugar, white	0 3	94 Kcals/1680 kJ
Whole-wheat bread	2.5	215 Kcals914 kJ	Chocolate, sweet	30.7	520 Kcals/2177 kJ
Cornflakes	0.7	360 Kcals/1535 kJ	Chocolate, semisweet	28	510 Kcals/2157 kJ
Raisin bran	1.6	303 Kcals/1289 kJ	Honey	0	288 Kcals/1229 kJ
Swiss-style granola	5.9	363 Kcals/1540 kJ	Lemon curd	5.0	283 Kcals/1198 kJ
Croissant	20.3	360 Kcals/1505 kJ	Fruit jam	0 26	268 Kcals/1114 kJ

FRUIT AND NUTS

	FAT (g)	ENERGY		FAT (g)	ENERGY
Apples	0.1	47 Kcals/199 kJ	Pears	0.1	40 Kcals/169 kJ
Avocados	19.5	190 Kcals/784 kJ	Almonds	55.8	612 Kcals/2534 kJ
Bananas	0.3	95 Kcals/403 kJ	Brazil nuts	68.2	682 Kcals/2813 kJ
Dried mixed fruit	0.4	268 Kcals/1114 kJ	Hazelnuts	63.5	650 Kcals/2685 kJ
Grapefruit	0.1	30 Kcals/126 kJ	Pine nuts	68.6	688 Kcals/2840 kJ
Oranges	0.1	37 Kcals/158 kJ	Walnuts	68.5	688 Kcals/2837kJ
Peaches	0.1	33 Kcals/142 kJ	Peanut butter, smooth	53.7	623 Kcals/2581 kJ

Soups
and Appetizers

ITALIAN VEGETABLE SOUP

The success of this clear soup depends on the quality of the stock, so for the best results be sure you use homemade vegetable stock rather than bouillon cubes.

INGREDIENTS

Serves 4
1 small carrot
1 baby leek
1 celery stalk
2oz green cabbage
3¾ cups vegetable stock
1 bay leaf
*1 cup cooked cannellini or
  navy beans*
*⅕ cup soup pasta, such as tiny shells,
  bows, stars or elbows*
salt and black pepper
chopped fresh chives, to garnish

1 Cut the carrot, leek and celery into 2in long julienne strips. Slice the cabbage very finely.

NUTRITION NOTES	
Per portion:	
Energy	69Kcals/288kJ
Protein	3.67g
Fat	0.71g
Saturated fat	0.05g
Fiber	2.82g

2 Put the stock and bay leaf into a large saucepan and bring to a boil. Add the carrot, leek and celery, cover and simmer for 6 minutes.

3 Add the cabbage, beans and pasta shapes. Stir, then simmer uncovered for another 4–5 minutes, or until the vegetables and pasta are tender.

4 Remove the bay leaf and season with salt and pepper to taste. Ladle into four soup bowls and garnish with chopped chives. Serve immediately.

CHICKEN AND PASTA SOUP

INGREDIENTS

Serves 4–6
3¾ cups chicken stock
1 bay leaf
4 scallions, sliced
8oz button mushrooms, sliced
4oz cooked chicken breast
2oz soup pasta
⅔ cup dry white wine
1 tablespoon chopped fresh parsley
salt and black pepper

NUTRITION NOTES	
Per portion:	
Energy	126Kcals/529kJ
Fat	2.2g
Saturated fat	0.6g
Cholesterol	19mg
Fiber	1.3g

1 Put the stock and bay leaf into a pan and bring to a boil.

2 Add the scallions and mushrooms to the stock.

3 Remove the skin from the chicken and slice the meat thinly, using a sharp knife. Add to the soup and season to taste. Heat thoroughly for 2–3 minutes.

4 Add the pasta, cover and simmer for 7–8 minutes. Just before serving, add the wine and chopped parsley, reheat for 2–3 minutes, then season to taste.

BEET SOUP WITH RAVIOLI

INGREDIENTS

Serves 4–6

*1 recipe basic pasta dough (see
    page 38)*
egg white, beaten, for brushing
flour, for dusting
1 small onion or shallot, finely chopped
2 garlic cloves, crushed
1 tsp fennel seeds
2½ cups chicken stock
8oz cooked beets
2 tablespoons fresh orange juice
fennel or dill leaves, to garnish
crusty bread, to serve

For the filling

1½ cups finely chopped mushrooms
1 shallot or small onion, finely chopped
1–2 garlic cloves, crushed
1 tsp chopped fresh thyme
1 tbsp chopped fresh parsley
6 tbsp fresh white breadcrumbs
salt and black pepper
large pinch of ground nutmeg

1 Process all the filling ingredients in a food processor or blender.

NUTRITION NOTES

Per portion:	
Energy	358Kcals/1504kJ
Fat	4.9g
Saturated fat	1.0g
Cholesterol	110mg
Fiber	4.3g

2 Roll the pasta dough into thin sheets. Lay one piece over a ravioli sheet and put a teaspoonful of the filling into each depression. Brush around the edges of each ravioli with egg white. Cover with another sheet of pasta, press the edges well together to seal and separate the individual shapes. Transfer to a floured dishtowel and let rest for 1 hour before cooking.

3 Cook the ravioli in a large pan of boiling salted water for 2 minutes, in batches, to keep them from sticking together. Remove and drop into a bowl of cold water for 5 seconds before placing on a tray. (You can make the pasta shapes a day in advance, if you like. Cover with plastic wrap and store in the fridge.)

4 Put the onion, garlic and fennel seeds into a pan with ⅔ cup of the stock. Bring to a boil, cover and simmer for 5 minutes until tender. Peel and finely dice the beets (reserve 4 tbsp for the garnish). Add the rest of the beets to the soup with the remaining stock and bring to a boil.

5 Add the orange juice and cooked ravioli and simmer for 2 minutes. Pour into shallow soup bowls and garnish with the reserved diced beets and fennel or dill leaves.

Spicy Tomato and Lentil Soup

Ingredients

Serves 4

1 tbsp sunflower oil
1 onion, finely chopped
1–2 garlic cloves, crushed
1in piece fresh ginger, peeled and
    finely chopped
1 tsp cumin seeds, crushed
1 lb ripe tomatoes, peeled, seeded and
    chopped
½ cup red split lentils
5 cups vegetable or chicken stock
1 tbsp tomato paste
salt and black pepper
low fat plain yogurt and chopped fresh
    parsley, to garnish (optional)

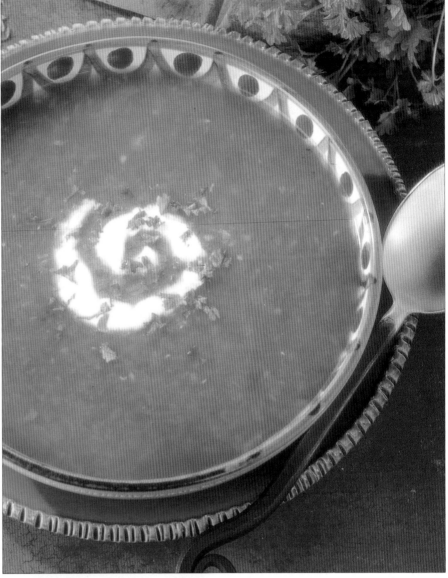

1 Heat the sunflower oil in a large heavy saucepan and cook the chopped onion gently for 5 minutes, until softened.

2 Stir in the garlic, ginger and cumin, followed by the tomatoes and lentils. Cook over low heat for another 3–4 minutes.

3 Stir in the stock and tomato paste. Bring to a boil, then lower the heat and simmer gently for about 30 minutes, until the lentils are soft. Season to taste with salt and pepper.

4 Purée the soup in a blender or food processor. Return to the clean pan and reheat gently. Serve in heated bowls. If desired, garnish each portion with a swirl of yogurt and a little chopped parsley.

NUTRITION NOTES	
Per portion:	
Energy	165Kcals/695kJ
Fat	4g
Saturated fat	0.5g
Cholesterol	0

CREAMY COD CHOWDER

A delicious light version of a classic, this chowder is a tasty combination of smoked fish, vegetables, fresh herbs and milk. To cut the calories and stock even more, use vegetable or fish stock in place of the milk. Serve as a substantial first course or snack, or as a light main meal accompanied by warm crusty whole-wheat bread.

INGREDIENTS

Serves 4–6
12oz smoked cod fillet
1 small onion, finely chopped
1 bay leaf
4 black peppercorns
3¾ cups skim milk
2 tsp cornstarch
7oz canned corn
1 tbsp chopped fresh parsley

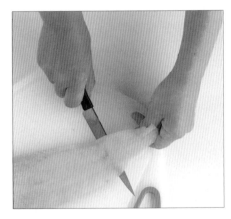

1 Skin the fish and put it into a large saucepan with the onion, bay leaf and peppercorns. Pour in the milk.

2 Bring to a boil, then reduce the heat and simmer very gently for 12–15 minutes, or until the fish is just cooked. Do not overcook.

3 Using a slotted spoon, lift out the fish and flake into large chunks. Remove the bay leaf and peppercorns and discard.

4 Blend the cornstarch with 2 tsp cold water and add to the pan. Bring to a boil and simmer for 1 minute or until slightly thickened.

5 Drain the corn and add to the saucepan with the flaked fish and parsley. Reheat gently and serve.

COOK'S TIP
The flavor of the chowder improves if it is made a day in advance. Allow to cool, then chill until just before you plan to serve. Reheat gently. Do not allow the soup to boil, or the fish will disintegrate.

NUTRITION NOTES

Per portion:

Energy	200Kcals/840kJ
Protein	24.71g
Fat	1.23g
Saturated fat	0.32g

MELON AND BASIL SOUP

A deliciously refreshing, chilled fruit soup, just right for a hot summer's day. It takes next to no time to prepare, leaving you free to enjoy the sunshine and, even better, it is almost totally fat-free.

INGREDIENTS

Serves 4–6
2 cantaloupes
6 tbsp sugar
¾ cup water
finely grated rind and juice of 1 lime
3 tablespoons shredded fresh basil
fresh basil leaves, to garnish

1 Cut the melons in half across the middle. Scrape out the seeds and discard. Using a melon baller, scoop out 20–24 balls and set aside for the garnish. Scoop out the remaining flesh and place in a blender or food processor. Set aside.

2 Place the sugar, water and lime zest in a small pan over low heat. Stir until dissolved, bring to a boil and simmer for 2–3 minutes. Remove from the heat and allow to cool slightly. Pour half the mixture into the blender or food processor with the melon flesh. Blend until smooth, adding the remaining syrup and lime juice to taste.

3 Pour the mixture into a bowl, stir in the basil and chill. Serve garnished with basil leaves and melon balls.

NUTRITION NOTES

Per portion:

Energy	69Kcals/293.8kJ
Fat	0.14g
Saturated fat	0
Cholesterol	0
Fiber	0.47g

COOK'S TIP
Add the syrup in two stages, because the amount of sugar needed will depend on the sweetness of the melon.

CHILLED FRESH TOMATO SOUP

This effortless uncooked soup can be made in minutes.

INGREDIENTS

Serves 6

3–3½ lb ripe tomatoes, peeled and
  coarsely chopped
4 garlic cloves, crushed
2 tbsp balsamic vinegar
4 thick slices whole-wheat bread
black pepper
low fat ricotta cheese, to garnish

1 Place the tomatoes in a blender with the garlic. Blend until smooth.

2 Press the mixture through a sieve to remove the seeds. Stir in the balsamic vinegar and season to taste with pepper. Put in the fridge to chill.

3 Toast the bread lightly on both sides. While still hot, cut off the crusts and slice the toast in half horizontally. Place on a board with the uncooked sides facing down and, using a circular motion, rub to remove any doughy pieces of bread.

COOK'S TIP
For the best flavor, it is important to use only fully-ripened, flavorful tomatoes in this soup.

4 Cut each slice into four triangles. Place on a broiler pan and toast the uncooked sides until lightly golden. Garnish each bowl of soup with a spoonful of ricotta cheese and serve with the Melba toast.

NUTRITION NOTES	
Per portion:	
Energy	111Kcals/475kJ
Fat	1.42g
Saturated fat	0.39g
Cholesterol	0.16mg
Fiber	4.16g

MINTED MELON AND GRAPEFRUIT

Melon is always a popular appetizer. Here the succulent flavor of the cantaloupe is complemented by the refreshing taste of citrus fruit and a simple mustard and vinegar dressing. Fresh mint, used in the cocktail and as a garnish, enhances both its flavor and appearance.

INGREDIENTS

Serves 4

1 cantaloupe, weighing about
  2¼lb
2 pink grapefruit
1 yellow grapefruit
1 tsp Dijon mustard
1 tsp raspberry or sherry vinegar
1 tsp honey
1 tbsp chopped fresh mint
a few sprigs of fresh mint,
  to garnish

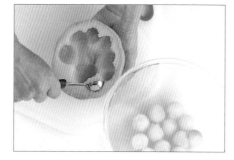

1 Halve the melon and remove the seeds with a teaspoon. With a melon baller, carefully scoop the flesh into balls.

NUTRITION NOTES

Per portion:	
Energy	97Kcals/409kJ
Protein	2.22g
Fat	0.63g
Saturated fat	0
Fiber	3.05g

2 With a small sharp knife, peel the grapefruit and remove all the white pith. Remove the segments by cutting between the membranes, holding the fruit over a small bowl to catch any juices.

3 Whisk the mustard, vinegar, honey, chopped mint and grapefruit juices together in a mixing bowl. Add the melon balls and the grapefruit and mix well. Chill for 30 minutes.

4 Ladle the fruit into four glass dishes and serve garnished with sprigs of fresh mint.

GUACAMOLE WITH CRUDITÉS

This fresh-tasting spicy dip is made using peas instead of the avocados that are traditionally associated with this dish. This version saves on both fat and calories, without compromising taste.

INGREDIENTS

Serves 4–6
2¼ cups frozen peas,
    defrosted
1 garlic clove, crushed
2 scallions, chopped
1 tsp finely grated rind and juice of 1
    lime
½ tsp ground cumin
dash of Tabasco sauce
1 tbsp reduced-fat mayonnaise
2 tbsp chopped cilantro
    or parsley
salt and black pepper
pinch of paprika and lime slices,
    to garnish

For the crudités
6 baby carrots
2 celery stalks
1 red-skinned eating apple
1 pear
1 tbsp lemon or lime juice
6 canned baby corns

2 Add the chopped cilantro or parsley and process for a few more seconds. Spoon into a serving bowl, cover with plastic wrap and chill in the fridge for 30 minutes, to let the flavors develop fully.

3 For the crudités, trim and peel the carrots. Halve the celery stalks lengthwise and trim into sticks, the same length as the carrots. Quarter, core and thickly slice the apple and pear, then dip into the lemon or lime juice. Arrange with the baby corn on a platter.

1 Put the peas, garlic clove, scallions, lime rind and juice, cumin, Tabasco sauce, mayonnaise and salt and black pepper into a food processor or a blender for a few minutes and process until smooth.

NUTRITION NOTES	
Per portion:	
Energy	110Kcals/460kJ
Protein	6.22g
Fat	2.29g
Saturated fat	0.49g
Fiber	6.73g

COOK'S TIP
Serve the guacamole with warmed whole-wheat pita bread.

4 Sprinkle the paprika over the guacamole and garnish with twisted lime slices.

TZATZIKI

Tzatziki is a Greek cucumber salad dressed with yogurt, mint and garlic. It is typically served with grilled lamb and chicken, but is also good served with crudités.

INGREDIENTS

Serves 4

1 cucumber
1 tsp salt
3 tbsp finely chopped fresh mint, plus a few sprigs to garnish
1 garlic clove, crushed
1 tsp sugar
1 cup low fat plain yogurt
cucumber flower, to garnish (optional)

1 Peel the cucumber. Reserve a little of the cucumber to use as a garnish if desired and cut the rest in half lengthwise. Remove the seeds with a teaspoon and discard. Slice the cucumber thinly and combine with salt. Let stand for 15–20 minutes. Salt will soften the cucumber and draw out any bitter juices.

COOK'S TIP
If you want to prepare Tzatziki in a hurry, then leave out the method for salting cucumber at the end of step 1. The cucumber will have a more crunchy texture, and will be slightly less sweet.

2 Combine the mint, garlic, sugar and yogurt in a bowl, reserving a few sprigs of mint as decoration.

3 Rinse the cucumber in a sieve under cold running water to remove the salt. Drain well and combine with the yogurt. Decorate with cucumber flower and/or mint. Serve cold.

NUTRITION NOTES	
Per portion:	
Energy	41.5Kcals/174.5kJ
Fat	0.51g
Saturated fat	0.25g
Cholesterol	2mg
Fiber	0.2g

CHILI TOMATO SALSA

This universal dip is great served with absolutely anything and can be made up to 24 hours in advance.

INGREDIENTS

Serves 4
1 shallot, peeled and halved
2 garlic cloves, peeled
handful of fresh basil leaves
1¼ lb ripe tomatoes
2 tsp olive oil
2 green chilies
salt and black pepper

1 Place the shallot and garlic in a food processor with the fresh basil. Blend the shallot, garlic and basil until finely chopped.

2 Halve the tomatoes and add to the food processor. Pulse the machine until the mixture is well blended and coarsely chopped.

3 With the motor running, slowly pour in the olive oil. Add salt and pepper to taste.

NUTRITION NOTES	
Per portion:	
Energy	28Kcals/79kJ
Fat	0.47g
Saturated fat	0.13g
Cholesterol	0
Fiber	1.45g

4 Halve the chilies lengthwise and remove the seeds. Finely slice the chilies across the width into tiny strips and stir into the tomato salsa. Serve at room temperature.

COOK'S TIP
The salsa is best made in the summer when tomatoes are at their best. In winter, use a drained 14oz can of plum tomatoes.

FRESH FIG, APPLE AND DATE SALAD

Sweet Mediterranean figs and dates combine especially well with crisp eating apples. A hint of almond serves to unite the flavors, but if you'd prefer to reduce the fat even more, omit the almond paste and add another 2 tablespoons low fat plain yogurt or use low fat ricotta cheese instead.

INGREDIENTS

Serves 4
6 large eating apples
juice of ½ lemon
6oz fresh dates
1oz almond paste
1 tsp orange-flower water
4 tbsp low fat plain yogurt
4 green or purple figs
4 almonds, toasted

1 Core the apples. Slice thinly, then cut into fine matchsticks. Moisten with lemon juice to keep them white.

NUTRITION NOTES

Per portion:
Energy	255Kcals/876.5kJ
Fat	4.98g
Saturated fat	505g
Cholesterol	2.25mg
Fiber	1.69g

2 Remove the pits from the dates and cut the flesh into fine strips, then combine with the apple slices.

3 Soften the almond paste with orange-flower water and combine with the yogurt. Mix well.

COOK'S TIP
For a slightly stronger almond flavor, add a few drops of almond extract to the yogurt mixture. When buying fresh figs, choose firm, unblemished fruit which give slightly when lightly squeezed. Avoid damaged, bruised or very soft fruit.

4 Pile the apples and dates in the center of four plates. Remove the stem from each of the figs and divide the fruit into quarters without cutting through the base. Squeeze the base with the thumb and forefinger of each hand to open up the fruit.

5 Place a fig in the center of each salad. Spoon the yogurt filling onto the figs and decorate each one with a toasted almond.

Vegetarian
Dishes

TAGLIATELLE WITH MUSHROOMS

INGREDIENTS

Serves 4

1 small onion, finely chopped
2 garlic cloves, crushed
⅔ cup vegetable stock
8oz mixed fresh mushrooms, such as portobello, oyster or chanterelles
4 tbsp white or red wine
2 tsp tomato paste
1 tbsp soy sauce
1 tsp chopped fresh thyme
2 tbsp chopped fresh parsley, plus extra to garnish
8oz fresh sun-dried tomato and herb tagliatelle
salt and black pepper
shavings of Parmesan cheese, to serve (optional)

1 Put the onion and garlic into a pan with the stock, then cover and cook for 5 minutes or until tender.

NUTRITION NOTES

Per portion:	
Energy	241Kcals/1010kJ
Fat	2.4g
Saturated fat	0.7g
Carbohydrate	45g
Fiber	3g

2 Add the mushrooms (quartered or sliced if large or left whole if small), wine, tomato paste and soy sauce. Cover and cook for 5 minutes.

3 Remove the lid from the pan and boil until the liquid has reduced by half. Stir in the chopped fresh herbs and season to taste.

4 Cook the fresh pasta in a large pot of boiling, salted water for 2–5 minutes, until *al dente*. Drain thoroughly and toss lightly with the mushrooms. Serve, garnished with parsley and shavings of Parmesan cheese, if desired.

PASTA PRIMAVERA

You can use any mixture of fresh, young spring vegetables to make this delicately flavored pasta dish.

INGREDIENTS

8oz thin asparagus spears, chopped in half
4oz snow peas, ends removed
4oz canned baby corn or fresh corn kernels
8oz whole baby carrots, trimmed
1 small red bell pepper, seeded and chopped
8 scallions, sliced
8oz torchietti or other pasta shapes
⅔ cup low fat cottage cheese
⅔ cup low fat yogurt
1 tbsp lemon juice
1 tbsp chopped parsley
1 tbsp chopped chives
skim milk (optional)
salt and black pepper
sun-dried tomato bread, to serve

1 Cook the asparagus spears in a pan of boiling, salted water for 3–4 minutes. Add the snow peas halfway through the cooking time. Drain and rinse both under cold water to stop further cooking.

2 Cook the corn, carrots, red pepper and scallions in the same way until tender. Drain and rinse.

3 Cook the pasta in a large pot of boiling, salted water according to the packet instruction, until *al dente*. Drain thoroughly.

4 Put the cottage cheese, yogurt, lemon juice, parsley, chives and seasoning into a food processor or blender and process until smooth. Thin the sauce with skim milk, if necessary. Put into a large pan with the pasta and vegetables, heat gently and toss carefully. Serve immediately with sun-dried tomato bread.

NUTRITION NOTES	
Per portion:	
Energy	320Kcals/1344kJ
Fat	3.1g
Saturated fat	0.4g
Cholesterol	3mg
Fiber	6.2g

SPAGHETTI WITH CHILI BEAN SAUCE

A nutritious vegetarian option, ideal as a low-fat main course.

INGREDIENTS

Serves 6

1 onion, finely chopped
1–2 garlic cloves, crushed
1 large green chili, seeded
  and chopped
⅔ cup vegetable stock
1 14oz can chopped tomatoes
2 tbsp tomato paste
½ cup red wine
1 tsp dried oregano
7 ounces green beans, sliced
1 14oz can red kidney
  beans, drained
1 14oz can cannellini
  beans, drained
1 14oz can chickpeas, drained
1 lb spaghetti
salt and black pepper

NUTRITION NOTES	
Per portion:	
Energy	431Kcals/1811kJ
Fat	3.6g
Saturated fat	0.2g
Cholesterol	0
Fiber	9.9g

1 To make the sauce, put the chopped onion, garlic and chili into a non-stick pan with the stock. Bring to a boil and cook for 5 minutes, until tender.

2 Add the tomatoes, tomato paste, wine, seasoning and oregano. Bring to a boil, cover and simmer the sauce for 20 minutes.

3 Cook the green beans in boiling, salted water for about 5–6 minutes, until tender. Drain thoroughly.

4 Add all the beans and the chickpeas to the sauce and simmer for another 10 minutes. Meanwhile, cook the spaghetti in a large pot of boiling, salted water according to the individual package instructions, until al dente. Drain thoroughly. Transfer the pasta to a serving dish or plates and top with the chili bean sauce.

COOK'S TIP
Rinse canned beans thoroughly under cold, running water to remove as much salt as possible, and drain well before use.

LENTIL BOLOGNESE

A really useful sauce to serve with pasta, as a pancake stuffing or even as a protein-packed sauce for vegetables.

INGREDIENTS

Serves 6
3 tbsp olive oil
1 onion, chopped
2 garlic cloves, crushed
2 carrots, coarsely grated
2 celery stalks, chopped
⅔ cup red lentils
1 14oz can chopped tomatoes
2 tbsp tomato paste
2 cups stock
1 tbsp fresh marjoram, chopped, or
   1 tsp dried marjoram
salt and black pepper

1 Heat the oil in a large saucepan and gently fry the onion, garlic, carrots and celery for about 5 minutes, until they are soft.

NUTRITION NOTES	
Per portion:	
Energy	103Kcals/432kJ
Fat	2.19g
Saturated fat	0.85g
Fiber	2.15g

2 Add the lentils, tomatoes, tomato paste, stock, marjoram and seasoning to the pan.

3 Bring the mixture to a boil, then partially cover with a lid and simmer for 20 minutes, until thick and soft. Use the sauce as required.

COOK'S TIP
You can easily reduce the fat in this recipe by using less olive oil, or substituting a little of the stock and cooking the vegetables over low heat in a non-stick frying pan until they are soft.

SWEET AND SOUR PEPPERS WITH PASTA

A tasty and colorful low fat dish – perfect for lunch or supper.

INGREDIENTS

Serves 4

1 red, 1 yellow and 1 orange bell pepper
1 garlic clove, crushed
2 tbsp capers
2 tbsp raisins
1 tsp whole-grain mustard
rind and juice of 1 lime
1 tsp honey
2 tbsp chopped cilantro
8oz pasta bows
salt and black pepper
shavings of Parmesan cheese, to serve
    (optional)

1 Quarter the peppers and remove the stalks and seeds. Put the quarters into boiling water and cook for 10–15 minutes, until tender. Drain and rinse under cold water, then peel off the skin and cut the flesh into strips lengthwise.

2 Put the garlic, capers, raisins, mustard, lime rind and juice, honey, cilantro and seasoning into a bowl and whisk together.

3 Cook the pasta in a large pot of boiling, salted water for 10–12 minutes, until al dente. Drain thoroughly.

4 Return the pasta to the pot and add the pepper strips and dressing. Heat gently, tossing to mix. Transfer to a warm serving bowl and serve with a few shavings of Parmesan cheese, if using.

NUTRITION NOTES	
Per portion:	
Energy	268Kcals/1125kJ
Fat	2.0g
Saturated fat	0.5g
Cholesterol	1.3mg
Fiber	4.3g

PASTA WITH CHICKPEA SAUCE

This is a delicious, and very speedy, low fat dish. The quality of canned beans and tomatoes is so good that it is possible to transform them into a very fresh-tasting pasta sauce in minutes. Choose whatever pasta shapes you like, although hollow shapes, such as penne (quills) or shells are particularly good with this sauce.

INGREDIENTS

Serves 6
1 lb penne or other pasta shapes
2 tsp olive oil
1 onion, thinly sliced
1 red bell pepper, seeded and sliced
1 14oz can chopped tomatoes
1 15oz can chickpeas
2 tbsp dry vermouth (optional)
1 tsp dried oregano
1 large bay leaf
2 tbsp capers
salt and black pepper
fresh oregano, to garnish

COOK'S TIP
Choose fresh or dried unfilled pasta for this dish. Whichever you choose, cook it in a large pot of water so that the pasta keeps separate and doesn't stick together. Fresh pasta takes 2–4 minutes to cook and dried pasta 8–10 minutes. Cook pasta until it is *al dente* – firm and neither too hard nor too soft.

NUTRITION NOTES

Per portion:
Energy	268Kcals/1125kJ
Fat	2.0g
Saturated fat	0.5g
Cholesterol	1.3mg
Fiber	4.3g

1 Boil the pasta as instructed on the package, then drain. Meanwhile, heat the oil in a large saucepan and gently fry the onion and pepper for about 5 minutes, stirring occasionally, until softened.

2 Add the tomatoes, chickpeas with their liquid, vermouth (if desired), herbs and capers and stir well.

3 Season to taste and bring to a boil, then simmer for about 10 minutes. Remove the bay leaf and mix in the pasta. Reheat and serve hot, garnished with sprigs of oregano.

PAPPARDELLE AND PROVENÇAL SAUCE

INGREDIENTS

Serves 4

2 small red onions
2/3 cup vegetable stock
1–2 garlic cloves, crushed
4 tbsp red wine
2 zucchini, cut in fingers
1 yellow bell pepper, seeded and sliced
1 14oz can tomatoes
2 tsp fresh thyme
1 tsp sugar
12oz pappardelle or other
   ribbon pasta
salt and black pepper
fresh thyme and 6 black olives, pitted
   and coarsely chopped, to garnish

NUTRITION NOTES	
Per portion:	
Energy	369Kcals/1550kJ
Fat	2.5g
Saturated fat	0.4g
Cholesterol	0
Fiber	4.3g

1 Cut each onion into eight wedges through the root end, to hold them together during cooking. Put into a saucepan with the stock and garlic. Bring to a boil, cover and simmer for 5 minutes, until tender.

2 Add the red wine, zucchini, yellow pepper, tomatoes, thyme, sugar and seasoning. Bring to a boil and cook gently for 5–7 minutes, shaking the pan occasionally to coat the vegetables with the sauce. (Do not overcook the vegetables. They are much nicer if they remain slightly crunchy.)

3 Cook the pasta in a large pot of boiling, salted water according to the package instructions, until *al dente*. Drain thoroughly.

4 Transfer the pasta to warmed serving plates and top with the vegetables. Garnish with fresh thyme and chopped black olives.

BASIC PASTA DOUGH
To make fresh pasta, sift 1 3/4 cups all-purpose flour and a pinch of salt onto a work surface and make a well in the center. Break two eggs into the well, and add 2 tsp cold water. Using a fork, beat the eggs gently, then gradually draw in the flour from the sides to make a thick paste. When the mixture becomes too stiff to use a fork, use your hands to mix to a firm dough. Knead for 5 minutes, until smooth. Wrap in plastic wrap and allow to rest for 20–30 minutes before rolling out and cutting.

BULGUR AND MINT SALAD

INGREDIENTS

Serves 4

1²⁄₃ cups bulgur
4 tomatoes
4 small zucchini, thinly sliced
   lengthwise
4 scallions, sliced on the diagonal
8 dried apricots, chopped
¼ cup raisins
juice of 1 lemon
2 tbsp tomato juice
3 tbsp chopped fresh mint
1 garlic clove, crushed
salt and black pepper
sprig of fresh mint, to garnish

1 Put the bulgur into a large bowl. Add enough boiling water to come 1in above the level of the wheat. Allow to soak for 30 minutes, then drain well and squeeze out any excess water in a clean dishtowel.

2 Meanwhile, plunge the tomatoes into boiling water for 1 minute and then into cold water. Slip off the skins. Halve, remove the seeds and cores and coarsely chop the flesh.

3 Stir the chopped tomatoes, zucchini, scallions, apricots and raisins into the bulgur.

4 Put the lemon and tomato juice, mint, garlic clove and seasoning into a small bowl and whisk together with a fork. Pour onto the salad and mix well. Chill for at least 1 hour. Serve garnished with a sprig of mint.

NUTRITION NOTES	
Per portion:	
Energy	293Kcals/1231kJ
Fat	1.69g
Saturated fat	0.28g
Fiber	2.25g

CHILI BEAN BAKE

The contrasting textures of sauce, beans, vegetables and a crunchy cornbread topping make this a memorable meal.

INGREDIENTS

Serves 4
1¼ cups red kidney beans
1 bay leaf
1 large onion, finely chopped
1 garlic clove, crushed
2 celery stalks, sliced
1 tsp ground cumin
1 tsp chili powder
1 14oz can chopped tomatoes
1 tbsp tomato paste
1 tsp dried mixed herbs
1 tbsp lemon juice
1 yellow bell pepper, seeded and diced
salt and black pepper
mixed salad, to serve

For the cornbread topping
1½ cups cornmeal
1 tbsp whole-wheat flour
1 tsp baking powder
1 egg, beaten
¾ cup skim milk

1 Soak the beans overnight in cold water. Drain and rinse well. Pour 4 cups water into a large, heavy saucepan, add the beans and bay leaf and boil rapidly for 10 minutes. Lower the heat, cover and simmer for 35–40 minutes or until the beans are tender.

NUTRITION NOTES

Per portion:	
Energy	399Kcals/1675kJ
Protein	22.86g
Fat	4.65g
Saturated fat	0.86g
Fiber	11.59g

2 Add the onion, garlic, celery, cumin, chili powder, chopped tomatoes, tomato paste and dried mixed herbs. Half cover the pan with a lid and simmer for another 10 minutes.

3 Stir in the lemon juice, yellow pepper and seasoning. Simmer for another 8–10 minutes, stirring occasionally, until the vegetables are just tender. Discard the bay leaf and spoon the mixture into a large casserole.

4 Preheat the oven to 425°F. To make the topping, put the cornmeal, flour, baking powder and a pinch of salt into a bowl and mix together. Make a well in the center and add the egg and milk. Mix and pour over the bean mixture. Bake for 20 minutes or until brown. Serve hot with mixed salad.

SPICY BEAN HOT POT

INGREDIENTS

Serves 4

3 cups button mushrooms
1 tbsp sunflower oil
2 onions, sliced
1 garlic clove, crushed
1 tbsp red wine vinegar
1 14oz can chopped tomatoes
1 tbsp tomato paste
1 tbsp Worcestershire sauce
1 tbsp whole-grain mustard
1 tbsp dark brown sugar
1 cup vegetable stock
1 14oz can red kidney beans,
    drained
1 14oz can cannellini beans,
    drained
1 bay leaf
$^1\!/_2$ cup raisins
salt and black pepper
chopped fresh parsley, to garnish

1 Wipe the mushrooms, then cut them into small pieces. Set aside.

2 Heat the oil in a large saucepan or flameproof casserole, add the onions and garlic and cook over low heat for 10 minutes until soft.

3 Add all the remaining ingredients except the mushrooms and seasoning. Bring to a boil, lower the heat and simmer for 10 minutes.

4 Add the mushrooms and simmer for 5 more minutes. Stir in salt and pepper to taste. Transfer to warm plates and sprinkle with parsley.

NUTRITION NOTES	
Per portion:	
Energy	280Kcals/1175kJ
Fat	4.5g
Saturated fat	0.5g
Cholesterol	0

RATATOUILLE PANCAKES

These pancakes are made slightly thicker than usual to hold the juicy vegetable filling. By using cooking spray, you can control the amount of fat you are using and keep it to a minimum.

INGREDIENTS

Serves 4
⅔ cup all-purpose flour
pinch of salt
¼ cup quick-cooking oatmeal
1 egg
1¼ cups skim milk
nonstick cooking spray
mixed salad, to serve

For the filling
1 large eggplant, cut into
  1in cubes
1 garlic clove, crushed
2 medium zucchini, sliced
1 green bell pepper, seeded and sliced
1 red bell pepper, seeded and sliced
5 tbsp vegetable stock
1 7oz can chopped tomatoes
1 teaspoon cornstarch
salt and black pepper

NUTRITION NOTES

Per portion:
Energy	182Kcals/767kJ
Protein	9.36g
Fat	3.07g
Saturated fat	0.62g
Fiber	4.73g

COOK'S TIP
Adding oatmeal to the batter mixture adds flavor, color and texture to the cooked pancakes. If desired, use whole-wheat flour in place of white flour to add extra fiber and flavor.

1 Sift the flour and a pinch of salt into a bowl. Stir in the oats. Make a well in the center, add the egg and half the milk and mix to a smooth batter. Gradually beat in the remaining milk. Cover the bowl and allow to stand for 30 minutes.

2 Spray a 7in heavy pan with cooking spray. Heat the pan, then pour in just enough batter to cover the bottom of the pan thinly. Cook for 2–3 minutes, until the underside is golden brown. Flip over and cook for another 1–2 minutes.

3 Slide the pancake out onto a plate lined with nonstick baking paper. Stack the other pancakes on top as they are made, interleaving each with parchment paper. Keep warm.

4 For the filling, put the eggplant in a colander and sprinkle well with salt. Let stand on a plate for 30 minutes. Rinse thoroughly and drain well.

5 Put the garlic clove, zucchini, peppers, stock and tomatoes into a large saucepan. Simmer uncovered, stirring occasionally, for 10 minutes. Add the eggplant and cook for another 15 minutes. Blend the cornstarch with 2 teaspoons water and stir into the saucepan. Simmer for 2 minutes. Season to taste.

6 Spoon some of the ratatouille mixture into the middle of each pancake. Fold each one in half, then in half again to make a cone shape. Serve hot with a mixed salad.

VEGETARIAN CASSOULET

Every town in southwest France has its own version of this popular classic. Warm French bread is all that you need to accompany this hearty low fat vegetable version.

INGREDIENTS

Serves 4–6
2 cups dried navy beans
1 bay leaf
2 onions
3 whole cloves
2 garlic cloves, crushed
1 tsp olive oil
2 leeks, thickly sliced
12 baby carrots
4oz button mushrooms
1 14oz can chopped tomatoes
1 tbsp tomato paste
1 tsp paprika
1 tbsp chopped fresh thyme
2 tbsp chopped fresh parsley
2 cups fresh white
   bread crumbs
salt and black pepper

NUTRITION NOTES

Per portion:
Energy	325Kcals/1378kJ
Fat	3.08g
Saturated Fat	0.46g
Cholesterol	0
Fiber	15.68g

COOK'S TIP
If you're short of time, use canned navy beans – you'll need two 14oz cans. Drain, reserving the bean juices and bring up to 1²/₃ cups with vegetable stock.

1 Soak the beans overnight in plenty of cold water. Drain and rinse under cold running water. Put them in a saucepan with 7½ cups of cold water and the bay leaf. Bring to a boil and cook rapidly for 10 minutes.

2 Peel one of the onions and spike with the cloves. Add to the beans, then reduce the heat. Cover and simmer gently for 1 hour, until the beans are almost tender. Drain, reserving the stock but discarding the bay leaf and onion.

3 Chop the remaining onion and put it into a large flameproof casserole together with the crushed garlic and olive oil. Cook gently for 5 minutes, or until softened.

4 Preheat the oven to 325°F. Add the leeks, carrots, mushrooms, chopped tomatoes, tomato paste, paprika and thyme to the casserole, then pour in about 1²/₃ cups of the reserved stock.

5 Bring to a boil, cover and simmer gently for 10 minutes. Stir in the cooked beans and parsley. Season to taste with salt and pepper.

6 Sprinkle the bread crumbs over the top and bake uncovered for 35 minutes, or until the topping is golden brown and crisp.

VEGETABLE BIRYANI

This exotic dish made from everyday ingredients will be appreciated by vegetarians and meat-eaters alike. It is extremely low in fat, but packed full of exciting flavors.

INGREDIENTS

Serves 4–6

1 cup long-grain rice
2 whole cloves
seeds of 2 cardamom pods
2 cups vegetable stock
2 garlic cloves
1 small onion, coarsely chopped
1 tsp cumin seeds
1 tsp ground coriander
½ tsp ground turmeric
½ tsp chili powder
1 large potato, peeled and cut into
 1in cubes
2 carrots, sliced
½ cauliflower, broken into florets
2oz green beans, cut into
 1in lengths
2 tbsp chopped cilantro
2 tbsp lime juice
salt and black pepper
sprig of cilantro, to garnish

NUTRITION NOTES	
Per portion:	
Energy	175Kcals/737kJ
Protein	3.66g
Fat	0.78g
Saturated fat	0.12g
Fiber	0.58g

COOK'S TIP
Substitute other vegetables, if you like. Zucchini, broccoli, parsnip and sweet potatoes would all be excellent choices.

4 Preheat the oven to 350°F. Spoon the spicy paste into a large flameproof casserole and cook over low heat for about 2 minutes, stirring occasionally.

5 Add the potato, carrots, cauliflower florets, beans and 6 tbsp water. Cover and cook over low heat for 12 more minutes, stirring occasionally. Add the chopped cilantro.

2 Reduce the heat, cover and simmer for 20 minutes, or until all the stock has been absorbed.

6 Remove the cloves and spoon the rice over the vegetables. Sprinkle with the lime juice. Cover and cook in the oven for 25 minutes, or until the vegetables are tender. Fluff up the rice with a fork before serving and garnish with a sprig of fresh cilantro.

1 Put the rice, cloves and cardamom seeds into a large, heavy saucepan. Pour in the stock and bring to a boil.

3 Meanwhile put the garlic cloves, onion, cumin seeds, coriander, ground turmeric, chili powder and seasoning into a blender or coffee grinder with 2 tablespoons water. Blend to a smooth paste.

Meat
and Poultry

BARBECUED CHICKEN

INGREDIENTS

Serves 4 or 8

8 small chicken pieces
2 limes, cut into wedges, 2 red chilies,
finely sliced, and 2 lemongrass stalks,
to garnish
rice, to serve

For the marinade
2 lemongrass stalks, chopped
1in piece fresh ginger
6 garlic cloves
4 shallots
½ bunch cilantro
1 tbsp sugar
½ cup coconut milk
2 tbsp fish sauce
2 tbsp soy sauce

COOK'S TIP
Don't eat the skin of the chicken –
it's only left on to keep the flesh
moist during cooking. Coconut
milk makes a good base for a
marinade or sauce, as it is low in
calories and fat.

NUTRITION NOTES

Per portion (for 8):

Energy	106Kcals/449kJ
Fat	2.05g
Saturated fat	1.10g
Cholesterol	1.10mg
Fiber	109g

1 To make the marinade, put all the ingredients into a food processor and process until smooth.

2 Put the chicken pieces in a dish and add the marinade. Set aside in a cool place to marinate for at least 4 hours or overnight.

3 Preheat the oven to 400°F. Put the chicken pieces on a rack on a baking tray. Brush the chicken with the marinade and bake for 20–30 minutes, or until the chicken is cooked and golden brown. Turn the pieces over halfway through cooking and brush with more marinade.

4 Garnish with lime wedges, finely sliced red chilies and lemongrass stalks. Serve with rice.

TANDOORI CHICKEN SKEWERS

This dish originates from the plains of the Punjab, at the foot of the Himalayas, where food is traditionally cooked in clay ovens known as tandoors – hence the name.

INGREDIENTS

Serves 4

4 boneless, skinless chicken breasts,
  about 3½oz each
1 tbsp lemon juice
3 tbsp tandoori paste
3 tbsp low fat plain yogurt
1 garlic clove, crushed
2 tbsp chopped cilantro
1 small onion, cut into wedges and
  separated into layers
1 tsp oil, for brushing
salt and black pepper
cilantro sprigs, to garnish
rice pilaf and nan, to serve

1 Chop the chicken breasts into 1in cubes, put in a bowl and add the lemon juice, tandoori paste, yogurt, garlic, cilantro and seasoning. Cover and let marinate in the fridge for 2–3 hours.

2 Preheat the broiler to high. Thread alternate pieces of chicken and onion onto four skewers.

COOK'S TIP
Use chopped, boned and skinned chicken thighs, or strips of turkey breasts, for a cheaper and equally low fat alternative.

3 Brush onions with a little oil, lay the skewers on a broiler rack and cook for 10–12 minutes, turning once.

4 Garnish the kebabs with cilantro and serve at once with rice pilaf and nan.

NUTRITION NOTES	
Per portion:	
Energy	215.7Kcals/91.2kJ
Fat	4.2g
Saturated fat	0.27g
Cholesterol	122mg
Fiber	0.22g

CHICKEN, CARROT AND LEEK PACKAGES

These intriguing packages may sound a bit fussy for everyday eating, but actually they take very little time, and you can freeze them so they'll be ready to cook when needed.

INGREDIENTS

Serves 4

4 *chicken fillets or skinless, boneless breasts*
2 *small leeks, sliced*
2 *carrots, grated*
2 *pitted black olives, chopped*
1 *garlic clove, crushed*
4 *anchovy fillets, halved lengthwise*
salt and black pepper
black olives and herb sprigs, to garnish

1 Preheat the oven to 400°F. Season the chicken well.

2 Cut out four sheets of lightly greased parchment paper about 9in square. Divide the leeks equally among them. Put a piece of chicken on top of each.

3 Stir together the carrots, olives and garlic. Season lightly and place on top of the chicken portions. Top each with two of the anchovy fillets.

4 Carefully wrap up each package, making sure the paper folds are sealed. Bake for 20 minutes and serve hot, in the paper, garnished with black olives and herb sprigs.

NUTRITION NOTES

Per portion:

Energy	154Kcals/651kJ
Fat	2.37g
Saturated fat	0.45g
Cholesterol	78.75mg
Fiber	2.1g

COOK'S TIP
Skinless, boneless chicken is low in fat and is an excellent source of protein. Small, skinless turkey breast fillets also work well in this recipe and make a tasty change.

RAGOÛT OF VEAL

If you are looking for a low-calorie dish to treat yourself – or some guests – then this is perfect, and quick, too.

INGREDIENTS

Serves 4

12oz veal cutlets or loin
2 tsp olive oil
10–12 tiny onions, kept whole
1 yellow bell pepper, seeded and
  cut into eighths
1 orange or red bell pepper, seeded
  and cut into eighths
3 tomatoes, peeled
  and quartered
4 fresh basil sprigs
2 tbsp dry vermouth or sherry
salt and black pepper

NUTRITION NOTES	
Per portion:	
Energy	158Kcals/665.5kJ
Fat	4.97g
Saturated Fat	1.14g
Cholesterol	63mg
Fiber	2.5g

1 Trim off any fat and cut the veal into cubes. Heat the oil in a frying pan and gently stir-fry the veal and onions until browned.

2 After a couple of minutes, add the peppers and tomatoes. Continue stir-frying for another 4–5 minutes.

> COOK'S TIP
> Lean beef or pork fillet may be used instead of veal, if you prefer. Shallots can replace the onions.

3 Add half the basil leaves, coarsely chopped (keep some for garnish), the vermouth or sherry, and seasoning. Cook, stirring frequently, for another 10 minutes, or until the meat is tender.

4 Sprinkle with the remaining basil leaves and serve hot.

THAI BEEF SALAD

A hearty salad of beef, laced with a chili and lime dressing.

INGREDIENTS

Serves 6
6 lean sirloin steaks, 3oz each
1 red onion, finely sliced
1/2 cucumber, finely sliced
  into matchsticks
1 lemongrass stalk, finely chopped
2 tbsp chopped scallions
juice of 2 limes
1–2 tbsp fish sauce
2–4 red chilies, finely sliced, to garnish
cilantro, Chinese mustard cress and
  mint leaves, to garnish

NUTRITION NOTES

Per portion:

Energy	101Kcals/424kJ
Fat	3.8g
Saturated fat	1.7g
Cholesterol	33.4mg
Fiber	0.28g

COOK'S TIP
Round or tenderloin steaks would work just as well in this recipe. Choose good-quality lean steaks and remove and discard any visible fat.

1 Broil the sirloin steaks until they are medium-rare, then allow to rest for 10–15 minutes.

2 When cool, thinly slice the beef and put the slices in a large bowl.

3 Add the sliced onion, cucumber matchsticks and lemongrass.

4 Add the scallions. Toss and season with lime juice and fish sauce. Serve at room temperature or chilled, garnished with the chilies, cilantro, mustard cress and mint.

THAI CHICKEN AND VEGETABLE STIR-FRY

INGREDIENTS

Serves 4

1 piece lemongrass (or the rind of
½ lemon)
½in piece fresh ginger
1 large garlic clove
2 tbsp sunflower oil
10oz lean chicken
½ red bell pepper, seeded and sliced
½ green bell pepper, seeded and sliced
4 scallions, chopped
2 medium carrots, cut into matchsticks
4oz thin green beans
1oz peanuts, lightly crushed
2 tbsp oyster sauce
pinch of sugar
salt and black pepper
cilantro leaves, to garnish
steamed rice, to serve

NUTRITION NOTES

Per portion:
Energy	106Kcals/449kJ
Fat	2.05g
Saturated fat	1.10g
Cholesterol	1.10mg
Fiber	109g

1 Thinly slice the lemongrass or lemon rind. Peel and chop the ginger and garlic. Heat the oil in a frying pan over high heat. Add the lemongrass or lemon rind, ginger and garlic, and stir-fry for 30 seconds, until brown.

2 Add the chicken and stir-fry for 2 minutes. Then add all the vegetables and stir-fry for 4–5 minutes, until the chicken is cooked and the vegetables are almost cooked.

3 Finally, stir in the peanuts, oyster sauce, sugar and seasoning to taste. Stir-fry for another minute to blend the flavors. Serve immediately, sprinkled with the cilantro leaves and accompanied by steamed rice.

COOK'S TIP
Make this quick supper dish a little hotter by adding more fresh ginger, if desired.

SPAGHETTI ALLA CARBONARA

This is a variation on the classic charcoal-burner's spaghetti, using turkey bacon and low fat cream cheese instead of the traditional bacon and egg.

INGREDIENTS

Serves 4
5oz smoked turkey bacon
oil, for frying
1 medium onion, chopped
1–2 garlic cloves, crushed
⅔ cup chicken stock
⅔ cup dry white wine
7oz low fat cream cheese
1 lb chili and garlic-flavored spaghetti
2 tbsp chopped fresh parsley
salt and black pepper
shavings of Parmesan cheese,
* to serve*

1 Cut the turkey bacon into ½in strips. Fry quickly in a nonstick pan for 2–3 minutes. Add the onion, garlic and stock to the pan. Bring to a boil, cover and simmer for about 5 minutes, until tender.

COOK'S TIP
If you can't find chili and garlic-flavored spaghetti, use plain spaghetti and add a small amount of fresh chili and garlic in step 4 or use the pasta of your choice.

2 Add the wine and boil rapidly until reduced by half. Whisk in the cream cheese and season to taste.

3 Meanwhile, cook the spaghetti in a large pot of boiling, salted water for 10–12 minutes, until *al dente*. Drain thoroughly.

4 Return the spaghetti to the pan with the sauce and parsley, toss well and serve immediately with a few thin shavings of Parmesan cheese.

NUTRITION NOTES	
Per portion:	
Energy	500Kcals/2102kJ
Fat	3.3g
Saturated fat	0.5g
Cholesterol	21mg
Fiber	4g

TURKEY AND PASTA BAKE

INGREDIENTS

Serves 4
10oz ground turkey
5oz smoked turkey bacon, chopped
1–2 garlic cloves, crushed
1 onion, finely chopped
2 carrots, diced
2 tbsp tomato paste
1¼ cups chicken stock
8oz rigatoni or penne pasta
2 tbsp grated Parmesan cheese
salt and black pepper

1 Brown the ground turkey in a non-stick saucepan, breaking up any large pieces with a wooden spoon, until well browned all over.

2 Add the chopped turkey bacon, garlic, onion, carrots, paste, stock and seasoning. Bring to a boil, cover and simmer for 1 hour, until tender.

3 Preheat the oven to 350°F. Cook the pasta in a large pot of boiling, salted water according to the package instructions, until *al dente*. Drain thoroughly and mix with the turkey sauce.

COOK'S TIP
Ground chicken or extra lean ground beef work just as well in this tasty recipe.

4 Transfer to a shallow ovenproof dish and sprinkle with grated Parmesan cheese. Bake for 20–30 minutes, until lightly browned on top.

NUTRITION NOTES

Per portion:
Energy	391Kcals/1641kJ
Fat	4.9g
Saturated fat	2.2g
Cholesterol	60mg
Fiber	3.5g

TURKEY AND TOMATO HOT POT

Here, turkey is turned into tasty meatballs in a rich tomato sauce.

INGREDIENTS

Serves 4
1 slice white bread, crusts removed
2 tbsp skim milk
1 garlic clove, crushed
$^1/_2$ tsp caraway seeds
8oz ground turkey
1 egg white
$1^1/_2$ cups chicken stock
1 14oz can tomatoes
1 tbsp tomato paste
$^1/_2$ cup quick-cooking rice
salt and black pepper
fresh basil, to garnish
carrot and zucchini ribbons, to serve

1 Cut the bread into small cubes and put into a mixing bowl. Sprinkle over the milk and allow to soak for 5 minutes.

2 Add the garlic clove, caraway seeds, turkey and seasoning to the bread. Stir well.

3 Whisk the egg white until stiff, then fold, half at a time, into the turkey mixture. Chill for 10 minutes.

4 While the turkey mixture is chilling, put the stock, tomatoes and tomato paste into a large saucepan and bring to a boil.

5 Add the rice, stir and cook briskly for about 5 minutes. Turn the heat down to a gentle simmer.

6 Meanwhile, shape the turkey mixture into 16 small balls. Carefully drop them into the tomato stock and simmer for another 8–10 minutes, or until both the turkey balls and rice are cooked. Garnish with basil, and serve with carrot and zucchini ribbons.

COOK'S TIPS
To make carrot and zucchini ribbons, cut the vegetables lengthwise into thin strips using a vegetable peeler, and blanch or steam until lightly cooked.

Lean ground turkey is low in fat and is a good source of protein. It makes an ideal base for this tasty low-fat supper dish. Use ground chicken in place of turkey for an appetizing alternative.

NUTRITION NOTES

Per portion:
Energy	190Kcals/798kJ
Protein	18.04g
Fat	1.88g
Saturated fat	0.24g
Fiber	10.4g

Fish
and Shellfish

CAJUN-STYLE COD

This recipe works equally well with any firm-fleshed fish – choose low fat fish, such as haddock or monkfish.

INGREDIENTS

Serves 4
4 cod steaks, about
  6oz each
2 tbsp low fat plain yogurt
1 tbsp lime or lemon juice
1 garlic clove, crushed
1 tsp ground cumin
1 tsp paprika
1 tsp mustard powder
½ tsp cayenne pepper
½ tsp dried thyme
½ tsp dried oregano
nonstick cooking spray
lemon slices, to garnish
new potatoes and a mixed green salad,
  to serve

NUTRITION NOTES	
Per portion:	
Energy	137Kcals/577kJ
Protein	28.42g
Fat	1.75g
Saturated fat	0.26g
Fiber	0.06g

1 Pat the fish dry with paper towels. Combine the yogurt and lime or lemon juice and brush lightly over both sides of the fish.

2 Stir together the crushed garlic, spices and herbs. Coat both sides of the fish with the seasoning mix, rubbing in well.

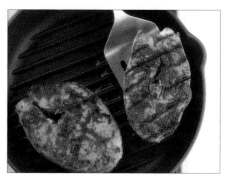

3 Spray a ridged broiler pan or heavy frying pan with nonstick cooking spray. Heat until very hot. Add the fish and cook over high heat for 4 minutes, or until the undersides are well browned.

4 Turn the steaks over and cook for another 4 minutes or until cooked through. Serve immediately, garnished with lemon and accompanied by new potatoes and a mixed salad.

FLOUNDER PROVENÇAL

INGREDIENTS

Serves 4

4 large flounder fillets
2 small red onions
½ cup vegetable stock
4 tbsp dry red wine
1 garlic clove, crushed
2 zucchini, sliced
1 yellow bell pepper, seeded and sliced
1 14oz can chopped tomatoes
1 tbsp chopped fresh thyme
salt and black pepper
potato gratin, to serve

1 Preheat the oven to 350°F. If necessary, skin the fish: lay the flounder skin-side down and, holding the tail end, push a sharp knife between the skin and flesh in a sawing motion. Hold the knife at a slight angle with the blade towards the skin.

2 Cut each onion into eight wedges. Place in a heavy saucepan with the stock. Cover and simmer for 5 minutes. Uncover and continue to cook, stirring occasionally, until the stock has evaporated. Add the wine and garlic clove to the pan and continue to cook until the onions are soft.

3 Add the zucchini, yellow pepper, tomatoes and thyme and season to taste. Simmer for 3 minutes. Spoon the sauce into a large casserole.

COOK'S TIP
Skinless white fish fillets such as flounder or sand dab are low in fat and make an ideal tasty and nutritious basis for many low-fat recipes such as this one.

4 Fold each fillet in half and put on top of the sauce. Cover and cook in the oven for 15–20 minutes, until the fish is opaque and flakes easily. Serve with a potato gratin.

NUTRITION NOTES
Per portion:

Energy	191Kcals/802kJ
Protein	29.46g
Fat	3.77g
Saturated fat	0.61g
Fiber	1.97g

MONKFISH AND MUSSEL SKEWERS

Skinless white fish such as monkfish is a good source of protein while also being low in calories and fat. These attractive seafood kebabs, flavored with a light marinade, are excellent broiled or barbecued and served with herbed boiled rice and a mixed green salad.

INGREDIENTS

Serves 4

1 lb monkfish, skinned and boned
1 tsp olive oil
2 tbsp lemon juice
1 tsp paprika
1 garlic clove, crushed
4 turkey bacon strips
8 cooked mussels
8 raw shrimp
1 tbsp chopped fresh dill
salt and black pepper
lemon wedges, to garnish
salad leaves and long-grain and wild
*   rice, to serve*

1 Cut the monkfish into 1in cubes and place in a shallow glass dish. Combine the oil, lemon juice, paprika and garlic. Season with pepper.

2 Pour the marinade over the fish and toss to coat evenly. Cover and put in a cool place for 30 minutes.

3 Cut the turkey bacon strips in half and wrap each strip around a mussel. Thread onto skewers, alternating with the fish cubes and raw shrimps. Preheat the broiler to high.

4 Broil the kebabs for 7–8 minutes, turning once and basting with the marinade. Sprinkle with chopped dill and salt. Garnish with lemon wedges and serve with salad and rice.

NUTRITION NOTES	
Per portion:	
Energy	133Kcals/560kJ
Protein	25.46g
Fat	3.23g
Saturated fat	0.77g
Fiber	0.12g

SOLE FILLETS BAKED IN A PAPER CASE

INGREDIENTS

Serves 4

4 sole or flounder fillets, about
  5 ounces each
½ small cucumber, sliced
4 lemon slices
4 tbsp dry white wine
sprigs of fresh dill, to garnish
potatoes and braised celery, to serve

For the yogurt hollandaise
½ cup low fat plain yogurt
1 tsp lemon juice
2 egg yolks
1 tsp Dijon mustard
salt and black pepper

1 Preheat the oven to 350°F. Cut out four heart shapes from nonstick parchment paper, each about 8 x 6 in.

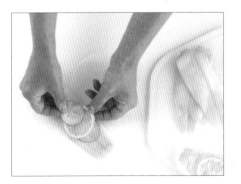

2 Place a sole fillet on one side of each paper heart. Arrange the cucumber and lemon slices on top of each fillet. Sprinkle with the wine and close the packages by turning the edges of the paper and twisting to secure. Put the packages on a baking sheet and cook for 15 minutes.

3 Meanwhile make the hollandaise. Beat together the yogurt, lemon juice and egg yolks in a double boiler or bowl placed over a saucepan. Cook over simmering water, stirring for about 15 minutes, or until thickened. (The sauce will become thinner after 10 minutes, but will thicken again.)

COOK'S TIP
Make sure that the paper packages are well sealed, so that none of the delicious juices can escape.

4 Remove from the heat and stir in the mustard. Season to taste with salt and pepper. Open the fish packages, garnish with a sprig of dill and serve accompanied with the sauce, new potatoes and braised celery.

NUTRITION NOTES	
Per portion:	
Energy	185Kcals/779kJ
Protein	29.27g
Fat	4.99g
Saturated fat	1.58g
Fiber	0.27g

STEAMED FISH WITH CHILI SAUCE

Steaming is one of the best – and lowest-fat – methods of cooking fish. By leaving the fish whole and on the bone, you'll find that all the delicious flavor and moistness is retained.

INGREDIENTS

Serves 6
1 large or 2 medium, firm fish like bass
   or grouper, scaled and cleaned
a fresh banana leaf or large piece
   of foil
2 tbsp rice wine
3 red chilies, seeded and finely sliced
2 garlic cloves, finely chopped
¾in piece of fresh ginger,
   finely shredded
2 lemongrass stalks, crushed and
   finely chopped
2 scallions, chopped
2 tbsp fish sauce
juice of 1 lime

For the chili sauce
10 red chilies, seeded and chopped
4 garlic cloves, chopped
4 tbsp fish sauce
1 tbsp sugar
5 tbsp lime juice

1 Rinse the fish under cold running water. Pat dry with paper towels. With a sharp knife, slash the skin of the fish a few times on both sides.

2 Place the fish on the banana leaf or foil. Combine the remaining ingredients and spread over the fish.

3 Place a small upturned plate in the bottom of a wok or large frying pan, and add about 2in boiling water. Lay the banana leaf or foil with the fish on top on the plate and cover with a lid. Steam for 10–15 minutes, or until the fish is cooked.

4 Meanwhile, put all the chili sauce ingredients in a food processor and process until smooth. You may need to add a little cold water to make the paste easier to process.

5 Serve the fish hot, on the banana leaf, if desired, with the sweet chili sauce to spoon over the top.

NUTRITION NOTES	
Per portion:	
Energy	170Kcals/721kJ
Fat	3.46g
Saturated fat	0.54g
Cholesterol	106mg
Fiber	0.35g

BAKED FISH IN BANANA LEAVES

Fish that is prepared in this way is particularly succulent and full of flavor. Fillets are used here, rather than whole fish, which is easier for those who don't like to mess with bones. It is a great dish for a barbecue.

INGREDIENTS

Serves 4

1 cup coconut milk
2 tbsp red curry paste
3 tbsp fish sauce
2 tbsp sugar
5 kafir lime leaves, torn
6oz fish fillets, such
    as snapper
6oz mixed vegetables, such as
    carrots or leeks, finely shredded
4 banana leaves or pieces of foil
2 tbsp shredded scallions,
    to garnish
2 red chilies, finely sliced, to garnish

NUTRITION NOTES

Per portion:

Energy	258Kcals/1094kJ
Fat	4.31g
Saturated fat	0.7g
Cholesterol	64.75mg
Fiber	1.23g

COOK'S TIP
Coconut milk is low in calories and fat and so makes an ideal basis for a low fat marinade or sauce. Choose colorful vegetables such as carrots, leeks and red bell pepper, to make the dish more attractive and appealing.

1 Combine the coconut milk, curry paste, fish sauce, sugar and kafir lime leaves in a shallow dish.

2 Marinate the fish in this mixture for 15–30 minutes. Preheat the oven to 400°F.

3 Lay a portion of the mixed vegetables on top of a banana leaf or piece of foil. Place a piece of fish on top with a little of its marinade.

4 Wrap the fish up by turning in the sides and ends of the leaf and secure with toothpicks. (With foil, just pinch the edges together.) Repeat with the rest of the fish.

5 Bake for 20–25 minutes or until the fish is cooked. Alternatively, cook under the broiler or on a barbecue. Just before serving, garnish the fish with a sprinkling of scallions and sliced red chilies.

HERBED FISHCAKES WITH LEMON SAUCE

The wonderful flavor of fresh herbs makes these fishcakes the catch of the day.

INGREDIENTS

Serves 4

12oz potatoes, coarsely chopped
5 tbsp skim milk
12oz haddock
  fillets, skinned
1 tbsp lemon juice
1 tbsp horseradish sauce
2 tbsp chopped fresh parsley
flour, for dusting
2 cups fresh whole-wheat bread crumbs
salt and black pepper
parsley sprigs, to garnish
sugar snap peas or snow peas and a
  sliced tomato and onion salad,
  to serve

For the lemon and chive sauce
thinly pared rind and juice of
  ½ small lemon
½ cup dry white wine
2 thin slices of fresh ginger
2 tsp cornstarch
2 tbsp chopped fresh chives

NUTRITION NOTES

Per portion:

Energy	232Kcals/975kJ
Protein	19.99g
Fat	1.99g
Saturated fat	0.26g
Fiber	3.11g

COOK'S TIP
Dry white wine is a tasty fat-free basis for this herb sauce. Try using cider as an alternative to wine, for a change.

1 Cook the potatoes in a large saucepan of boiling water for 15–20 minutes. Drain and mash with the milk and season to taste.

2 Purée the fish together with the lemon juice and horseradish sauce in a blender or food processor. Mix with the potatoes and parsley.

3 With floured hands, shape the mixture into eight fishcakes and coat with the breadcrumbs. Chill in the fridge for 30 minutes.

4 Preheat the grill to medium and cook the fishcakes for 5 minutes on each side, until browned.

5 To make the sauce, cut the lemon rind into julienne strips and put into a large saucepan together with the lemon juice, wine and ginger. Season to taste with salt and pepper.

6 Simmer, uncovered, for about 6 minutes. Blend the cornstarch with 1 tbsp of cold water, add to the pan and simmer until clear. Stir in the chives immediately before serving.

7 Serve the sauce hot with the fishcakes, garnished with parsley sprigs and accompanied by peas and a tomato and onion salad.

MEDITERRANEAN FISH FILLETS

These low fat fish fillets are nicely complemented by boiled potatoes, broccoli and carrots.

INGREDIENTS

Serves 4

4 white fish fillets, about
   5oz each
⅓ cup fish stock or dry white wine (or
   a mixture of the two), for poaching
1 bay leaf, a few black peppercorns
   and a strip of pared lemon rind, for
   flavoring
chopped fresh parsley, to garnish

For the tomato sauce

1 14oz can chopped tomatoes
1 garlic clove, crushed
1 tbsp pastis or other anise-
   flavored liqueur
1 tbsp drained capers
12–16 pitted black olives
salt and black pepper

1 To make the sauce, place the chopped tomatoes, garlic, pastis, capers and olives in a saucepan. Season to taste with salt and pepper and cook over low heat for about 15 minutes, stirring occasionally.

2 Place the fish in a frying pan, pour over the stock and/or wine and add the bay leaf, peppercorns and lemon rind. Cover and simmer for 10 minutes or until it flakes easily.

3 Using a slotted spoon, transfer the fish into a heated dish. Strain the stock into the tomato sauce and boil to reduce slightly. Season the sauce, pour it over the fish and serve immediately, sprinkled with the chopped parsley.

COOK'S TIP
Remove skin from cutlets and reduce the quantity of olives to reduce calories and fat. Use 1 lb fresh tomatoes, skinned and chopped, in place of the canned tomatoes.

NUTRITION NOTES

Per portion:

Energy	165Kcals/685kJ
Fat	3.55g
Saturated fat	0.5g
Cholesterol	69mg

BAKED COD WITH TOMATOES

For the very best flavor, use firm sun-ripened tomatoes for the sauce and make sure it is fairly thick before spooning it over the cod.

INGREDIENTS

Serves 4
2 tsp olive oil
1 onion, chopped
2 garlic cloves, finely chopped
1 lb tomatoes, peeled, seeded
    and chopped
1 tsp tomato paste
4 tbsp dry white wine
4 tbsp chopped flat leaf parsley
4 cod steaks
2 tbsp dried bread crumbs
salt and black pepper
new potatoes and green salad, to serve

NUTRITION NOTES

Per portion:	
Energy	151Kcals/647kJ
Fat	1.5g
Saturated fat	0.2g
Cholesterol	55.2mg
Fiber	2.42g

COOK'S TIP
For extra speed, use a 14oz can of chopped tomatoes in place of the fresh tomatoes and 1–2 tsp prepared minced garlic in place of the garlic cloves.

1 Preheat the oven to 375°F. Heat the oil in a pan and fry the onion for about 5 minutes. Add the garlic, tomatoes, tomato paste, wine and seasoning.

2 Bring the sauce just to a boil, then reduce the heat slightly and cook, uncovered, for 15–20 minutes, until thick. Stir in the parsley.

3 Grease an ovenproof dish, put in the cod cutlets and spoon an equal amount of the tomato sauce onto each. Sprinkle the dried bread crumbs over the top.

4 Bake for 20–30 minutes, basting the fish occasionally with the sauce, until the fish is tender and cooked through, and the bread crumbs are golden and crisp. Serve hot with new potatoes and a green salad.

Vegetable
Side Dishes

Herb Baked Tomatoes

Ingredients

Serves 4–6

1½ lb large red and yellow
   tomatoes
2 tsp red wine vinegar
½ tsp whole-grain mustard
1 garlic clove, crushed
2 tsp chopped fresh parsley
2 tsp chopped fresh chives
½ cup fresh fine white
   bread crumbs, for topping
salt and black pepper

Nutrition Notes

Per portion:	
Energy	37Kcals/156kJ
Fat	0.49g
Saturated fat	0.16g
Cholesterol	0
Fiber	1.36g

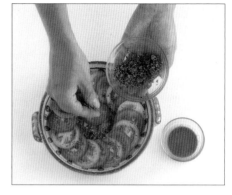

1 Preheat the oven to 400°F. Thickly slice the tomatoes and arrange half of them in a 4 cup ovenproof casserole.

Cook's Tip
Use whole-wheat bread crumbs in place of white, for added color, flavor and fiber. Use 1–2 tsp mixed dried herbs, if fresh herbs are not available.

---

2 Mix the vinegar, mustard, garlic and seasoning together. Stir in 2 teaspoons cold water. Sprinkle the tomatoes with half the parsley and chives, then drizzle with half the dressing.

3 Lay the remaining tomato slices on top, overlapping them slightly. Drizzle with the remaining dressing.

4 Sprinkle with the bread crumbs. Bake for 25 minutes or until the topping is golden. Sprinkle with the remaining parsley and chives. Serve immediately, garnished with sprigs of parsley.

POTATO GRATIN

The flavor of Parmesan is wonderfully strong, so a little goes a long way. Leave the cheese out altogether for an almost fat-free dish.

INGREDIENTS

Serves 4
1 garlic clove
5 large baking potatoes, peeled
3 tbsp freshly grated Parmesan cheese
2½ cups vegetable or chicken stock
pinch of grated nutmeg
salt and black pepper

1 Preheat the oven to 400°F. Halve the garlic clove and rub the cut surface over the base and sides of a large shallow gratin dish.

2 Slice the potatoes very thinly and arrange a third of them in the dish. Sprinkle with a little grated Parmesan cheese, and season with salt and pepper. Pour on some of the stock to prevent the potatoes from discoloring.

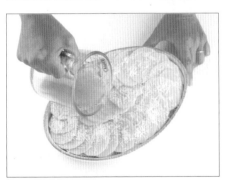

3 Continue layering the potatoes and cheese as before, then add the rest of the stock. Sprinkle with the grated nutmeg.

COOK'S TIP
For a potato and onion gratin, thinly slice one medium onion and layer with the potato.

4 Bake in the preheated oven for 1¼–1½ hours, or until the potatoes are tender and the tops well browned.

NUTRITION NOTES	
Per portion:	
Energy	178Kcals/749kJ
Protein	9.42g
Fat	1.57g
Saturated fat	0.30g
Fiber	1.82g

Baked Garlic Potatoes

With a low fat topping these would make a superb meal in themselves or could be enjoyed as a nutritious accompaniment to grilled fish or meat.

Ingredients

Serves 4

4 baking potatoes
2 garlic cloves, cut into slivers
4 tbsp low fat ricotta cheese
4 tbsp low fat plain yogurt
2 tbsp snipped chives
6–8 watercress sprigs, finely chopped
(optional)

Nutrition Notes	
Per portion:	
Energy	195Kcals/815kJ
Fat	3.5g
Saturated fat	2g
Cholesterol	10mg

1 Preheat the oven to 400°F. Slice each potato at about ¼in intervals, cutting not quite to the base, so that they retain their shape. Slip the slivers of the garlic between the cuts in the potatoes.

Cook's Tip
If available, farmer's cheese or low fat cream cheese are very good substitutes for the ricotta cheese.

2 Place the garlic-filled potatoes in a roasting tin and bake for 1–1¼ hours, or until soft when tested with a knife. Meanwhile, mix the low fat ricotta cheese and yogurt in a bowl, then stir in the snipped chives, along with the watercress, if using.

3 Serve the baked potatoes on individual plates, with a dollop of the yogurt and ricotta cheese mixture on top of each.

Potato, Leek and Tomato Tian

Ingredients

Serves 4

1½ lb potatoes
2 leeks, sliced
3 large tomatoes, sliced
a few fresh rosemary sprigs, crushed
1 garlic clove, crushed
1¼ cups vegetable stock
1 tbsp olive oil
salt and black pepper

Nutrition Notes	
Per portion:	
Energy	180Kcals/740kJ
Fat	3.5g
Saturated fat	0.5g
Cholesterol	0

1 Preheat the oven to 350°F and grease a 5-cup shallow ovenproof dish. Scrub and thinly slice the potatoes. Alternately layer them with the leeks and tomatoes in the dish, sprinkling some rosemary between the layers and ending with a layer of potatoes.

2 Add the garlic to the stock, stir in salt if needed and pepper to taste, then add to the vegetables. Brush the top layer of potatoes with olive oil.

3 Bake for 1¼–1½ hours, until the potatoes are tender and the topping is golden and slightly crisp.

ZUCCHINI IN CITRUS SAUCE

If baby zucchini are unavailable, you can use larger ones, but they should be cooked whole, so that they don't absorb too much water. After cooking, halve them lengthwise and cut into 4-inch lengths. These tender, baby zucchini served in a very low fat sauce make this a tasty and low fat accompaniment to grilled fish fillets.

NUTRITION NOTES	
Per portion:	
Energy	33Kcals/138kJ
Protein	2.18g
Fat	0.42g
Saturated fat	0.09g
Fiber	0.92g

INGREDIENTS

Serves 4
12oz baby zucchini
4 scallions, finely sliced
1in piece fresh ginger, grated
2 tbsp cider vinegar
1 tbsp light soy sauce
1 tsp light brown sugar
3 tbsp vegetable stock
finely grated rind and juice of ½ lemon
    and ½ orange
1 tsp cornstarch

1 Cook the zucchini in lightly salted boiling water for 3–4 minutes or until just tender. Drain well.

2 Meanwhile, put all the remaining ingredients, except the cornstarch, into a small saucepan and bring to a boil. Simmer for 3 minutes.

3 Blend the cornstarch with 2 tsp cold water and add to the sauce. Bring to a boil, stirring constantly, until the sauce has thickened.

4 Pour the sauce over the zucchini and heat gently, shaking the pan to coat them evenly. Transfer to a warmed serving dish and serve.

COOK'S TIP
Use baby corn or eggplant in place of the zucchini for an appetizing change.

ZUCCHINI AND ASPARAGUS PACKAGES

To appreciate the aroma, these paper packages should be broken open at the table.

INGREDIENTS

Serves 4
2 medium zucchini
1 medium leek
8oz young asparagus, trimmed
4 tarragon sprigs
4 whole garlic cloves, unpeeled
1 egg, beaten, to glaze
salt and black pepper

NUTRITION NOTES	
Per portion:	
Energy	110Kcals/460kJ
Protein	6.22g
Fat	2.29g
Saturated fat	0.49g
Fiber	6.73g

1 Preheat the oven to 400°F. Using a potato peeler, carefully slice the zucchini lengthwise into thin strips.

2 Cut the leek into very fine julienne strips and cut the asparagus evenly into 2in lengths.

3 Cut out four sheets of parchment paper measuring 12 x 15 in and fold in half. Draw a large curve to make a heart shape when unfolded. Cut along the inside of the line and open out.

4 Divide the zucchini, asparagus and leek evenly between each paper heart, positioning the filling on one side of the fold line, and topping each with a sprig of tarragon and an unpeeled garlic clove. Season to taste.

5 Brush the edges lightly with the beaten egg and fold over.

6 Twist the edges together so that each package is completely sealed. Lay the packages on a baking sheet and cook for 10 minutes. Serve immediately.

COOK'S TIP
Experiment with other vegetable combinations, if desired.

VEGETABLES À LA GRECQUE

This simple side salad is made with winter vegetables, but you can vary it according to the season. This combination of vegetables makes an ideal, low fat side salad to serve with grilled lean meat or poultry, or with thick slices of fresh, crusty bread.

INGREDIENTS

Serves 4

¾ cup white wine
1 tsp olive oil
2 tbsp lemon juice
2 bay leaves
sprig of fresh thyme
4 juniper berries
1 lb leeks, cut into 1in lengths
1 small cauliflower, broken into florets
4 celery stalks, sliced on the diagonal
2 tbsp chopped fresh parsley
salt and black pepper

1 Put the wine, oil, lemon juice, bay leaves, thyme and juniper berries into a large, heavy saucepan and bring to a boil. Cover and let simmer for 20 minutes.

NUTRITION NOTES	
Per portion:	
Energy	88Kcals/368kJ
Protein	4.53g
Fat	2.05g
Saturated fat	0.11g
Fiber	4.42g

2 Add the leeks, cauliflower and celery. Simmer very gently for 5–6 minutes, or until just tender.

3 Remove the vegetables with a slotted spoon and transfer them to a serving dish. Briskly boil the cooking liquid for 15–20 minutes, or until reduced by half. Strain.

4 Stir the parsley into the liquid and season with salt and pepper to taste. Pour over the vegetables and allow to cool. Chill in the fridge for at least 1 hour before serving.

COOK'S TIP
Choose a dry or medium-dry white wine for best results.

ROASTED MEDITERRANEAN VEGETABLES

For a really colorful dish, try these vegetables roasted in olive oil with garlic and rosemary. The flavor is wonderfully intense.

INGREDIENTS

Serves 6
1 each red and yellow bell pepper
2 Spanish onions
2 large zucchini
1 large eggplant or 4 baby eggplant, trimmed
1 fennel bulb, thickly sliced
2 beefsteak tomatoes
8 fat garlic cloves
2 tbsp olive oil
fresh rosemary sprigs
black pepper
lemon wedges and black olives (optional), to garnish

1 Halve and seed the peppers, then cut them into large chunks. Peel the onions and cut into thick wedges.

NUTRITION NOTES

Per portion:
Energy	120Kcals/504kJ
Fat	5.2g
Saturated fat	0.68g
Cholesterol	0

2 Cut the zucchini and eggplant into large chunks.

3 Preheat the oven to 425°F. Spread the peppers, onions, zucchini, eggplant and fennel in a lightly oiled shallow ovenproof dish or roasting pan, or, if desired, arrange in rows to make a colorful design.

4 Cut each tomato in half and place, cut-side up, with the vegetables.

5 Tuck the garlic cloves among the vegetables, then brush them with the olive oil. Place some sprigs of rosemary among the vegetables and grind some black pepper over the top, particularly on the tomatoes.

6 Roast for 20–25 minutes, turning the vegetables halfway through the cooking time. Serve from the dish or on a flat platter, garnished with lemon wedges. Scatter some black olives over the top, if desired.

Desserts

BAKED APPLES IN HONEY AND LEMON

A classic mix of flavors in a healthy, traditional family dessert. Serve warm, with skim-milk pudding or low fat frozen yogurt.

INGREDIENTS

Serves 4
4 medium cooking apples
1 tbsp honey
grated rind and juice of 1 lemon
1 tbsp low fat margarine
low fat frozen yogurt, to serve

1 Preheat the oven to 350°F. Remove the cores from the apples, leaving them whole.

NUTRITION NOTES	
Per portion:	
Energy	61Kcals/259.5kJ
Fat	1.62g
Saturated fat	0.42g
Cholesterol	0.25mg

2 With a sharp knife, cut lines through the apple skin at intervals, then arrange the apples in an oven-proof dish.

3 Combine the honey, lemon rind, juice and low fat margarine.

4 Spoon the mixture into the apples and cover the dish with foil or a lid. Bake for 40–45 minutes, or until the apples are tender. Serve with frozen yogurt.

APPLE AND BLACK CURRANT PANCAKES

These pancakes are made with a whole-wheat batter and are filled with a delicious fruit mixture.

INGREDIENTS

Makes 10

1 cup whole-wheat flour
1¼ cups skim milk
1 egg, beaten
1 tbsp sunflower oil, plus extra for
  greasing
low fat crème fraîche, to serve
  (optional)
toasted nuts or sesame seeds, for
  sprinkling (optional)

For the filling
1 lb cooking apples
8oz black currants
2–3 tbsp water
2 tbsp raw sugar

1 To make the pancake batter, put the flour in a mixing bowl and make a well in the center.

2 Add a little of the milk with the egg and the oil. Beat the flour into the liquid, then gradually beat in the rest of the milk, keeping the batter smooth and free from lumps. Cover the batter and chill while you prepare the filling.

COOK'S TIP
If you wish, substitute other combinations of fruit for apples and black currants.

3 Quarter, peel and core the apples. Slice them into a pan and add the black currants and water. Cook over low heat for 10–15 minutes until the fruit is soft. Stir in enough raw sugar to sweeten.

NUTRITION NOTES	
Per portion:	
Energy	120Kcals/505kJ
Fat	3g
Saturated fat	0.5g
Cholesterol	25mg

4 Lightly grease a nonstick pan with just a smear of oil. Heat the pan, pour in about 2 tablespoons of the batter, swirl it around and cook for about 1 minute. Flip the pancake over with a spatula and cook the other side. Put on a piece of paper towel and keep hot while cooking the remaining pancakes.

5 Fill the pancakes with the apple and black currant mixture and roll them up. Serve with a dollop of crème fraîche, if using, and sprinkle with nuts or sesame seeds, if desired.

CINNAMON AND APRICOT SOUFFLÉS

Don't expect these to be difficult simply because they're soufflés – they really couldn't be easier, and, best of all, they're very low in calories.

INGREDIENTS

Serves 4
3 eggs
½ cup apricot fruit spread
finely grated rind of ½ lemon
1 tsp ground cinnamon
extra cinnamon, to decorate

NUTRITION NOTES

Per portion:
Energy	102Kcals/429kJ
Fat	4.97g
Saturated fat	1.42g
Cholesterol	176.25mg
Fiber	0

1 Preheat the oven to 375°F. Lightly grease four individual soufflé dishes and dust them lightly with flour.

2 Separate the eggs and put the yolks in a bowl with the fruit spread, lemon rind and cinnamon.

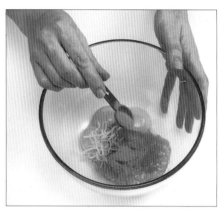

3 Whisk hard until the mixture is thick and pale in color.

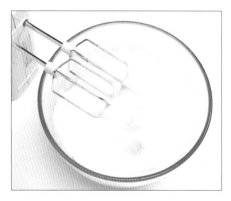

4 Place the egg whites in a clean bowl and whisk them until they are stiff enough to hold soft peaks.

5 Using a large metal spoon or spatula, fold the egg whites evenly into the yolk mixture.

6 Divide the soufflé mixture between the prepared dishes and bake for 10–15 minutes, until well risen and golden brown. Serve immediately, dusted with a little extra cinnamon.

COOK'S TIP
Puréed fresh or well-drained canned fruit can be used instead of the apricot spread, but make sure the mixture is not too wet, or the soufflés will not rise properly.

BLUEBERRY AND ORANGE CRÊPE BASKETS

Impress your guests with these pretty, fruit-filled crêpes. When blueberries are out of season, replace them with other soft fruit, such as raspberries.

INGREDIENTS

Serves 6
1¼ cups all-purpose flour
pinch of salt
2 egg whites
⅞ cup skim milk
⅔ cup orange juice
oil, for frying
low fat yogurt, to serve
For the filling
4 medium oranges
2 cups blueberries

1 Preheat the oven to 400°F. To make the crêpes, sift the flour and salt into a bowl. Make a well in the center and add the egg whites, milk and orange juice. Whisk hard, until all the liquid has been incorporated and the batter is smooth and bubbly.

2 Lightly grease a heavy or nonstick pancake pan and heat it until it is very hot. Pour in just enough batter to cover the bottom of the pan, swirling it to cover the pan evenly.

3 Cook the crêpe over medium-high heat until the crêpe has set and is golden, then turn it to cook the other side. Remove the crêpe to a piece of paper towel. Cook the remaining batter in the same way to make 6–8 crêpes.

4 Place six small ovenproof bowls or molds on a baking sheet and lay the crêpes over these. Bake them in the oven for about 10 minutes, until they are crisp and set into shape. Lift the "baskets" off the molds.

5 Pare a thin piece of orange rind from one orange and cut it into fine strips. Blanch the strips in boiling water for 30 seconds, rinse them in cold water and set them aside. Cut all the peel and white pith from the oranges.

6 Divide the oranges into segments, catching the juice, combine with the blueberries and warm them gently. Spoon the fruit into the baskets and scatter the rind over the tops. Serve with yogurt.

COOK'S TIP
Don't fill the crêpe baskets until you're ready to serve them, because they will absorb the fruit juice and begin to soften.

NUTRITION NOTES

Per portion:

Energy	157.3Kcals/668.3kJ
Fat	2.20g
Saturated fat	0.23g
Cholesterol	0.66mg
Fiber	2.87g

FILO CHIFFON PIE

Filo pastry is low in fat and is very easy to use. Keep a package in the freezer, ready to make impressive desserts like this one.

INGREDIENTS

Serves 6
1¼ lb rhubarb
1 tsp pumpkin pie spice
finely grated rind and juice of 1 orange
1 tbsp granulated sugar
1 tbsp butter
3 filo pastry sheets

1 Preheat the oven to 400°F. Wash the rhubarb, then trim and cut it into 1in pieces and put them in a bowl.

2 Add the pumpkin pie spice, orange rind and juice and sugar. Transfer the rhubarb to a 4-cup pie dish.

NUTRITION NOTES

Per portion:

Energy	71Kcals/299kJ
Fat	2.5g
Saturated fat	1.41g
Cholesterol	5.74mg
Fiber	1.48g

3 Melt the butter and brush it over the pastry. Lift the pastry onto the pie dish, butter-side up, and crumple it up decoratively to cover the pie.

> VARIATION
> Other fruit can be used in this pie – just prepare depending on type.

4 Put the dish on a baking sheet and bake for 20 minutes, until golden brown. Reduce the heat to 350°F and bake for another 10–15 minutes, until the rhubarb is tender.

CRUNCHY FRUIT LAYER

INGREDIENTS

Serves 2

1 peach or nectarine
1 cup crunchy granola with nuts
²⁄₃ cup low fat plain yogurt
1 tbsp jam
1 tbsp fruit juice

NUTRITION NOTES

Per portion:

Energy	240Kcals/1005kJ
Fat	3g
Saturated fat	1g
Cholesterol	3mg

1 Remove the pit from the peach or nectarine and cut the fruit into bite-size pieces with a sharp knife.

2 Divide the chopped fruit between two tall glasses, reserving a few pieces for decoration.

3 Sprinkle the granola over the fruit in an even layer, then top with the low fat yogurt.

4 Stir the jam and the fruit juice together in a cup, then drizzle the mixture over the yogurt. Decorate with the reserved peach or nectarine pieces and serve immediately.

ICED ORANGES

The ultimate fat-free treat – these delectable orange sherbets served in fruit shells were originally sold in beach cafés in the south of France.

INGREDIENTS

Serves 8
⅔ cup sugar
juice of 1 lemon
14 medium oranges
8 fresh bay leaves, to decorate

NUTRITION NOTES	
Per portion:	
Energy	139Kcals/593kJ
Fat	0.17g
Saturated fat	0
Cholesterol	0
Fiber	3g

COOK'S TIP
Use crumpled paper towels to keep the shells upright.

1 Put the sugar in a heavy saucepan. Add half the lemon juice, then add ½ cup water. Cook over low heat until the sugar has dissolved. Bring to a boil and boil for 2–3 minutes, until the syrup is clear.

2 Slice the tops off eight of the oranges to make "hats." Scoop out the flesh of the oranges and reserve. Freeze the empty orange shells and "hats" until needed.

3 Grate the rind of the remaining oranges and add to the syrup. Squeeze the juice from the oranges, and from the reserved flesh. There should be 3 cups. Squeeze another orange or add bought orange juice, if necessary.

4 Stir the orange juice and remaining lemon juice, with 6 tablespoons water, into the syrup. Taste, adding more lemon juice or sugar as desired. Pour the mixture into a shallow freezer container and freeze for 3 hours.

5 Turn the orange sherbet mixture into a bowl and whisk thoroughly to break up the ice crystals. Freeze for 4 hours more, until firm, but not solid.

6 Pack the mixture into the hollowed-out orange shells, mounding it up, and set the "hats" on top. Freeze the sherbet shells until ready to serve. Just before serving, make a hole with a skewer in the tops of the "hats" and push in a bay leaf, to decorate.

RASPBERRY VACHERIN

Meringue rounds filled with orange-flavored low fat cream cheese and fresh raspberries make this a perfect dinner party dessert.

INGREDIENTS

Serves 6
3 egg whites
¾ cup superfine sugar
1 tsp chopped almonds
confectioners' sugar, for dusting
raspberry leaves, to decorate (optional)

For the filling
¾ cup low fat cream cheese
1–2 tbsp honey
1–2 tbsp Cointreau
½ cup low fat ricotta
  or farmer's cheese
8oz raspberries

NUTRITION NOTES	
Per portion:	
Energy	197Kcals/837.5kJ
Fat	1.02g
Saturated fat	0.36g
Cholesterol	1.67mg
Fiber	1g

COOK'S TIP
When making the meringue, whisk the egg whites until they are so stiff that you can turn the bowl upside-down without their falling out.

1 Preheat the oven to 275°F. Draw an 8in circle on two pieces of non-stick parchment paper. Turn the paper over so the marking is on the underside and use it to line two heavy baking sheets.

2 Whisk the egg whites in a clean bowl until very stiff, then gradually whisk in the superfine sugar to make a stiff meringue mixture.

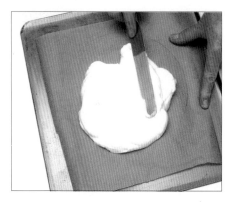

3 Spoon the mixture onto the circles on the prepared baking sheets, spreading the meringue evenly to the edges. Sprinkle one meringue round with the chopped almonds.

4 Bake for 1½–2 hours or until crisp and dry, then carefully lift the meringue rounds off the baking sheets. Peel away the paper and cool the meringues on a wire rack.

5 To make the filling, cream the soft cheese with the honey and liqueur in a bowl. Gradually fold in the ricotta cheese and the raspberries, reserving three berries for decoration.

6 Place the plain meringue round on a board, spread with the filling and top with the nut-covered round. Dust with the confectioners' sugar, transfer to a serving plate and decorate with the reserved raspberries and a sprig of raspberry leaves, if desired.

Tropical Yogurt Ring

An impressive, light and colorful tropical dessert with a truly fruity flavor.

Ingredients

Serves 6
For the yogurt ring
¾ cup tropical fruit juice
1 envelope powdered gelatin
3 egg whites
1 cup low fat plain yogurt
finely grated rind of 1 lime

For the filling
1 mango
2 kiwi fruit
½ cup raspberries
juice of 1 lime

1 Place the tropical fruit juice in a small pan and sprinkle on the powdered gelatin. Heat gently until the gelatin has dissolved.

2 Whisk the egg whites in a clean, dry bowl until they hold soft peaks. Continue whisking hard, while gradually adding the yogurt and lime rind.

3 Continue whisking hard and pour in the hot gelatin and the egg white and yogurt mixture in a steady stream, until everything is smooth and evenly mixed.

4 Quickly pour the mixture into a 6 cup ring mold. Chill the mold in the fridge until set. The mixture will separate into two layers.

5 Halve, pit, peel and dice the mango. Peel and slice the kiwi fruit. Pick over the raspberries carefully. Toss all the fruits together and stir in the lime juice.

6 Run a knife around the edge of the ring to loosen the mixture. Dip the mold quickly into cold water and then turn the chilled yogurt mold out onto a serving plate. Spoon all the prepared fruit into the center of the ring and serve immediately.

Nutrition Notes

Per portion:	
Energy	83.5Kcals/355kJ
Fat	0.67g
Saturated fat	0.27g
Cholesterol	2.16mg
Fiber	1.77g

Cook's Tip
Any mixture of fruit works in this recipe, depending on the season. In summer try using apple juice in the ring mixture and fill it with luscious, red summer fruits.

Index